AF261458

ROMAN ART

Author: Eugenie Strong and Elie Faure

Layout:
Baseline Co. Ltd,
District 10, Ho Chi Minh City
Vietnam

ISBN: 978-1-68325-935-0

Printed in

Eugenie Strong and Elie Faure

ROMAN ART

Architecture, sculpture, and the empire's legacy

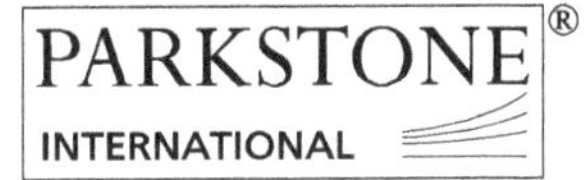

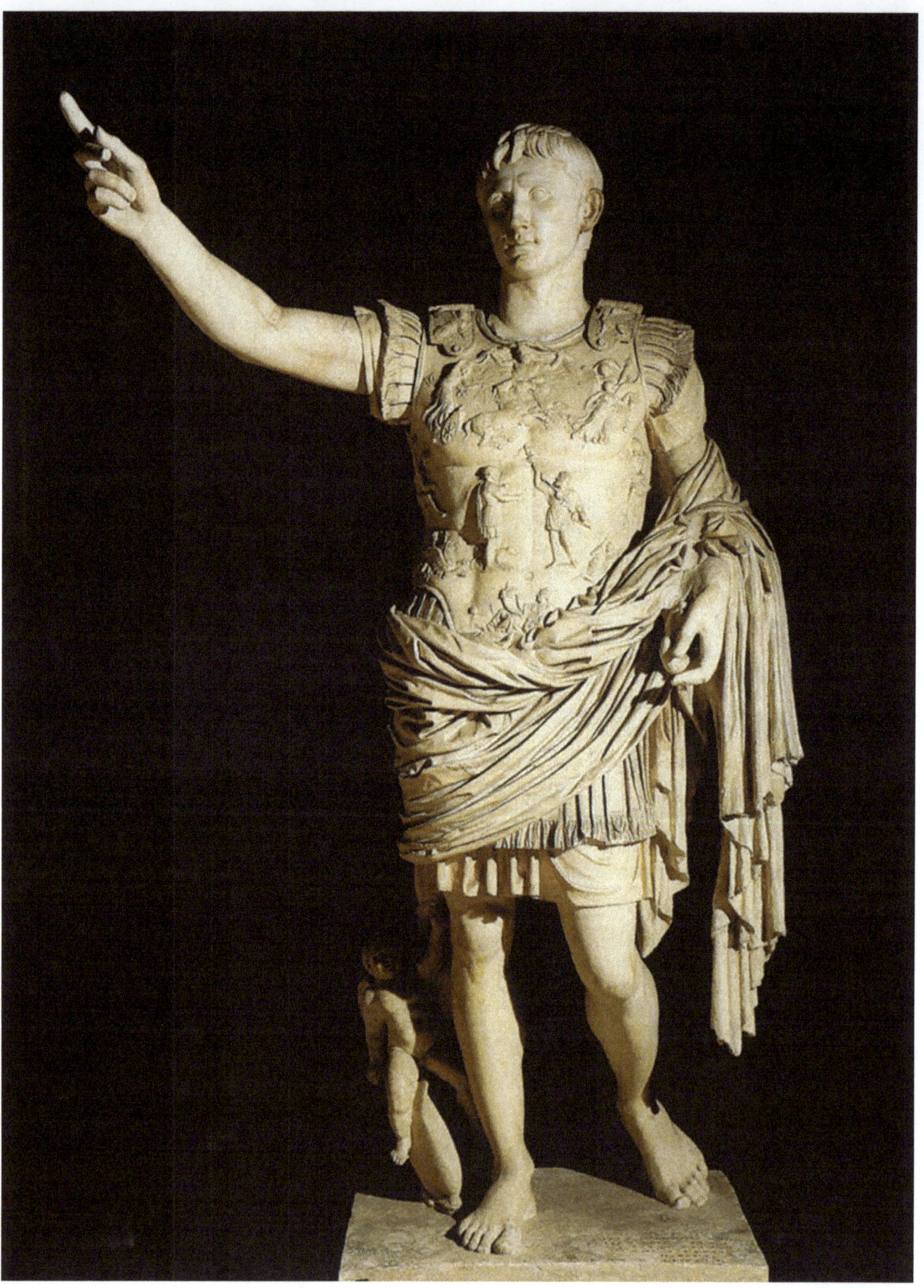

CONTENTS

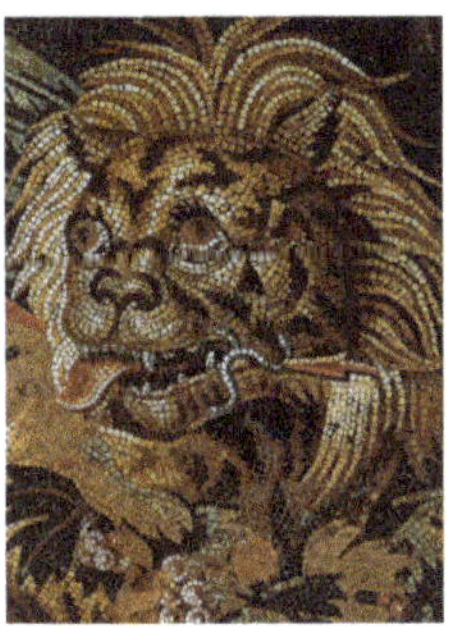

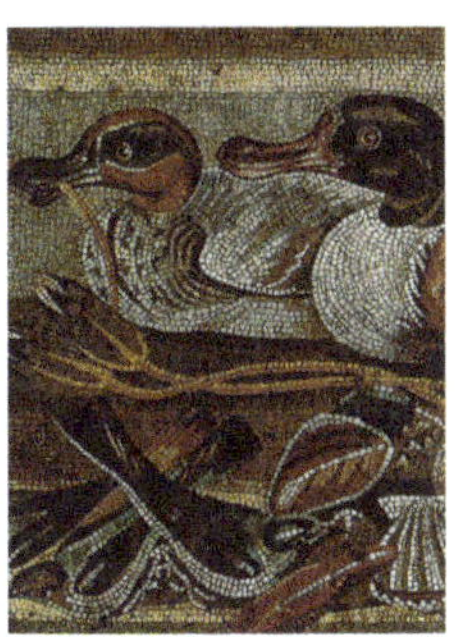

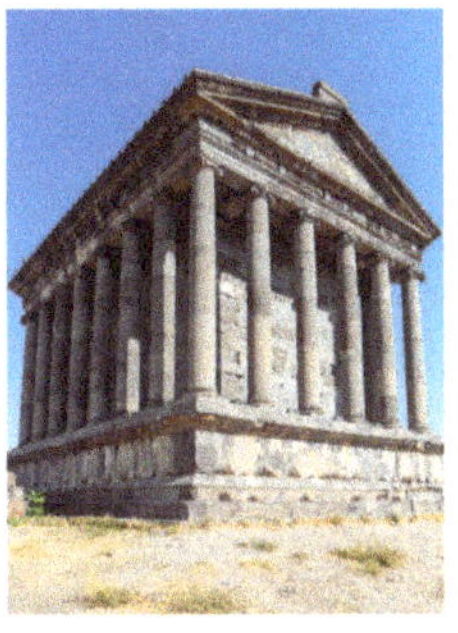

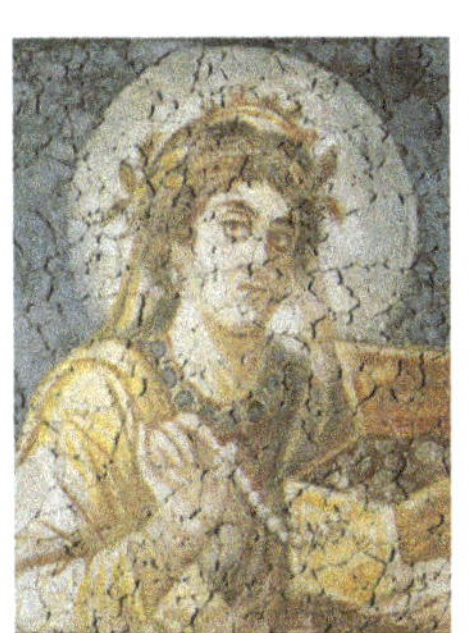

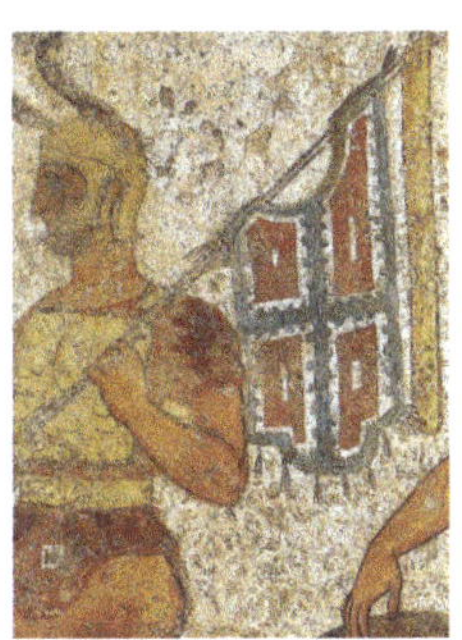

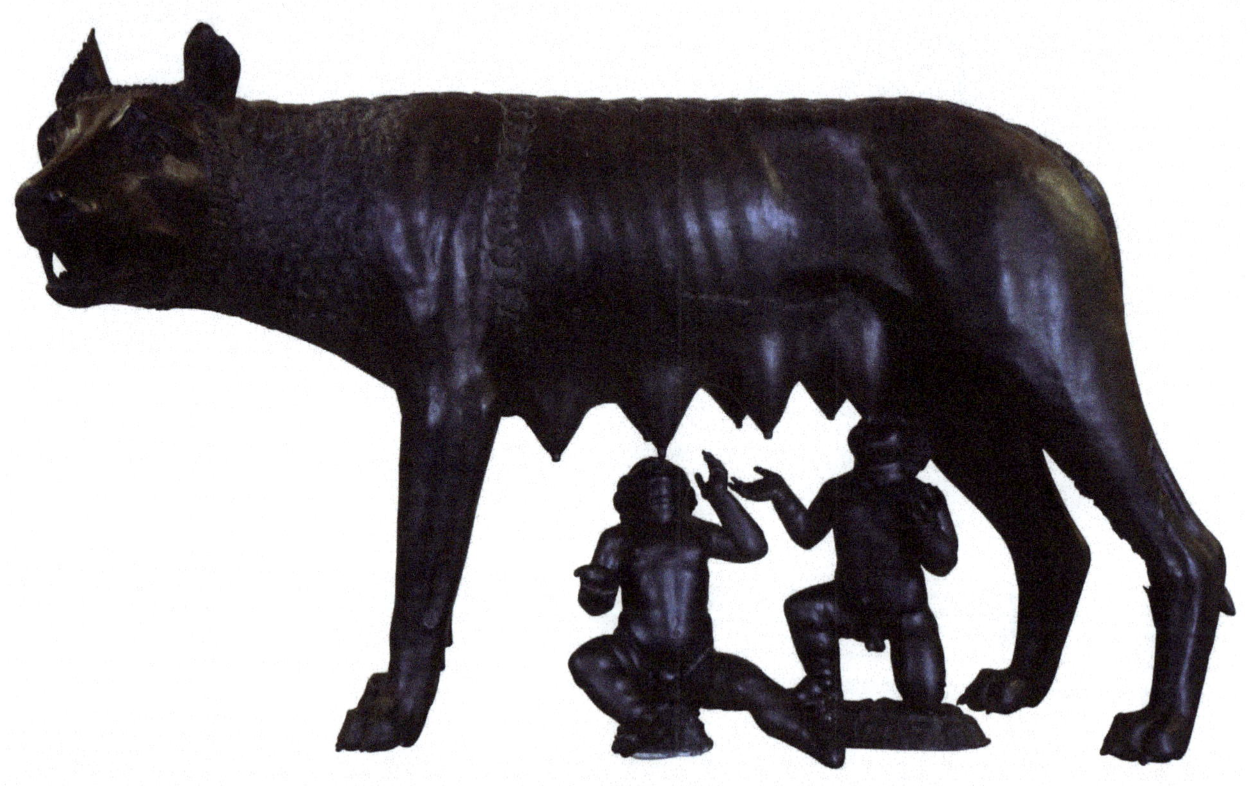

INTRODUCTION

Roman art has its origin in the national character and circumstances of the Romans. The prevalent emotions and the ideas of a nation are expressed in its art, and some of these emotions and ideas are peculiar to the national character, while some are produced by the national circumstances. In order to criticize the faults into which Roman art was liable to fall we had better begin by tracing the ideal to which they aspired, and then show how these aspirations were checked or modified.

Cicero's writings show that he valued a mental ideal as the highest point to which art could reach. The Romans as well as the Greeks ascribed it to a divine inspiration. Horace distinctly says that the Greeks derived their powers of poetic art from the Muses, and the Romans thought that they received it from the gods and what they valued most was imperial power:

▲ *Statue of Augustus*. Prima Porta, Villa de Livia, 20 B.C. Marble, H: 2.06 m. Rome, Musei Vaticani

◀ *The Wolf of the Capitol*, breastfeeding the twins Remus and Romulus. Bronze Sculpture from the beginning of the 5th century BC. (Infants date from the Renaissance). Rome.

The ideal in matters of taste was only derived by them from the gods through the medium of another nation. Their own notion of the highest of all things, their *summum bonum*, was not the beautiful, but the powerful. And this they thought they had as a nation received from heaven.

It is often hastily concluded that Roman art is not worth our attention. The Romans, it is said, were evidently a nation devoid of the spiritual grace and noble power wherewith the Greeks earned the admiration of the world, by having produced everlasting types of beauty in art. And it must be acknowledged that, from a strictly accurate artistic point of view, this is in a great measure true.

The more lofty spirits among the Romans no doubt lifted themselves above the atmosphere in which they were compelled to live, because they had studied the great writers of Greek philosophy. Hence, Cicero says, as before mentioned, that more beautiful images can be conceived in the mind than seen by the eye:

And he goes on in a passage which is often quoted to say that even more beautiful statues or pictures than the best which we know can be imagined in the mind. We must therefore except such men as Cicero from our general criticism of

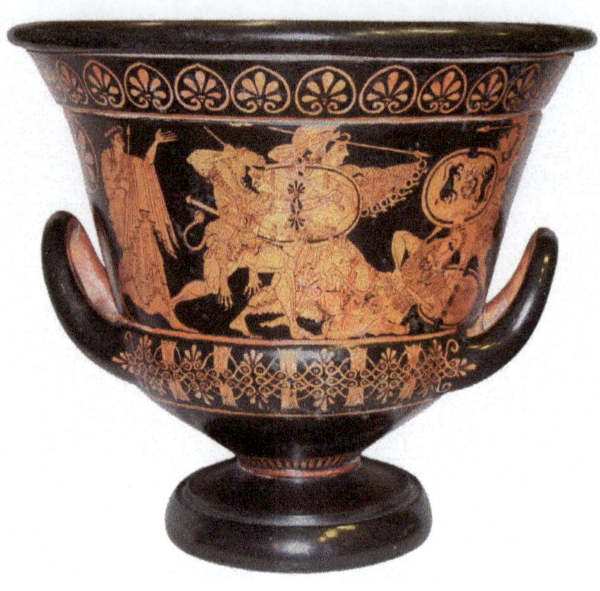

▲ *Amphora* realized by Euphronio VI century BC

the Romans. Nor must we deny lofty aspirations to Roman poets. Horace in his Ars Poetica strikes this principal chord at once when he calls on the poet to avoid selfish pride in his own powers and to aim higher.

This was always done by the artists who raised Greek art to its highest level. They began with an appeal to their gods, and by their brilliant po wers of generalisation and idealisation soared above into a supernatural region. We have elsewhere remarked that the Iliad begins, as Horace advises, with a prayer to the Muse, while the Aeneid breaks this rule and throws all the weight on the poet's shoulders, as if he were competent to bear it, and could ascend into a spiritual atmosphere without looking beyond himself. Spiritual thought as one of the highest attributes of man is mentioned in one of Sophocles's most beautiful choruses.

The lofty aim of art among the Greeks was not pursued far by the Romans, who contented themselves with a practical and realistic view of fine art and made their Emperor the highest ideal to which they rose. Hence Roman sculpture to a great extent employed itself in deifying men. The influence of the Christian faith at a later time gradually raised this old grovelling Roman materialism; but sculpture among the Romans never soared high, and painting took the place of sculpture in spiritualising art. Thus there has been no great Christian sculptor to compare with the great Christian painters, and the chief development of the Christian influence on art, besides painting, has been in the great cathedral architecture which has elevated and enlarged human thought in so many of the great cities of Europe. The characteristic tone of materialism which we see pervading all ancient Roman work, is diametrically opposed to this spiritual and upward tendency expressed by Gothic architecture, and we are therefore prepared to find Roman art deadening the elevated tone of Christianity for many centuries.

Orange, South face of the Arc de Triomphe. ▶
According to Pierre Gros, the arch has been built to honor Germanicus in the aftermath of his death in 19 A.D., and again to honor Tiberius, in 26-27 A.D.

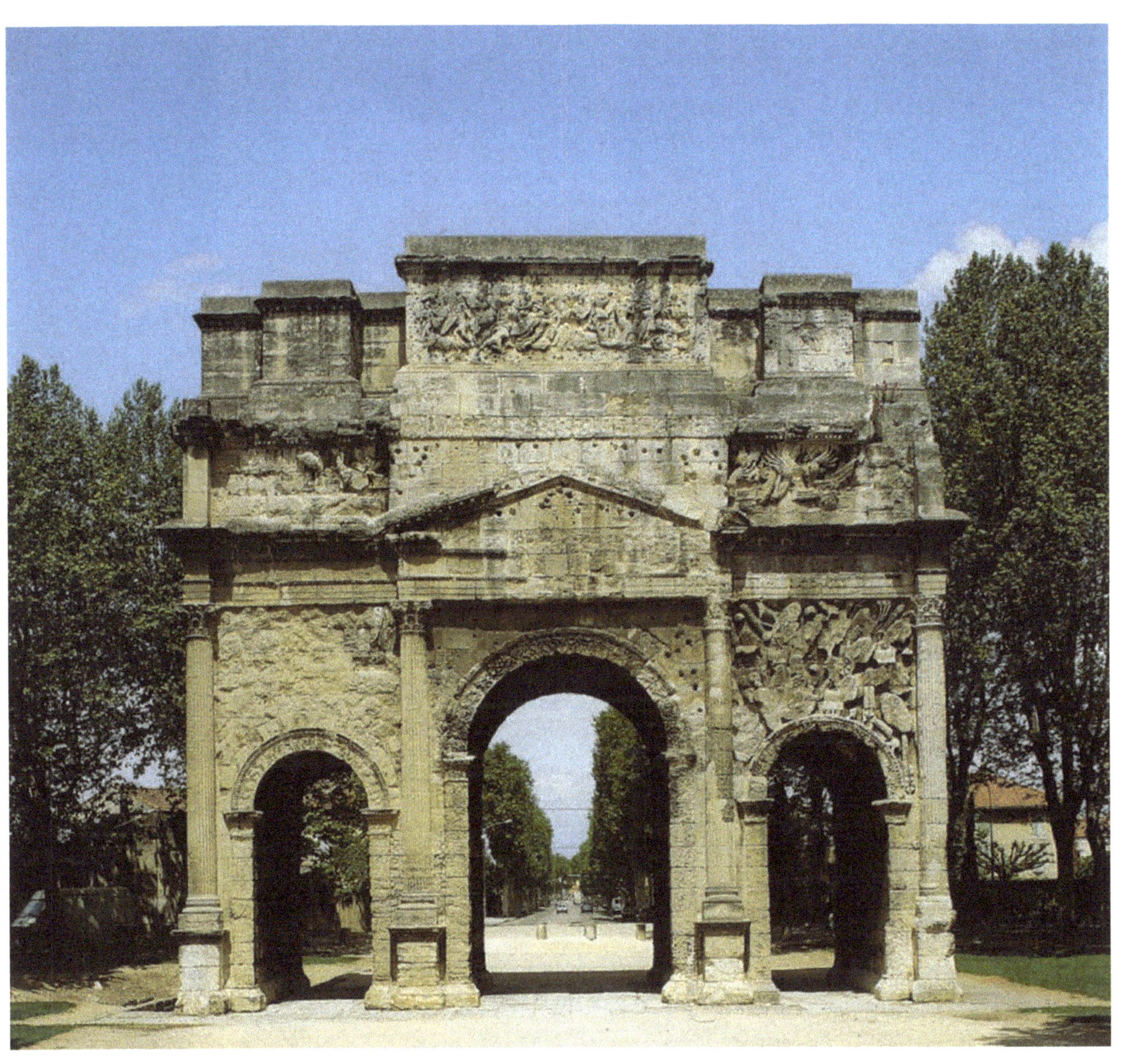

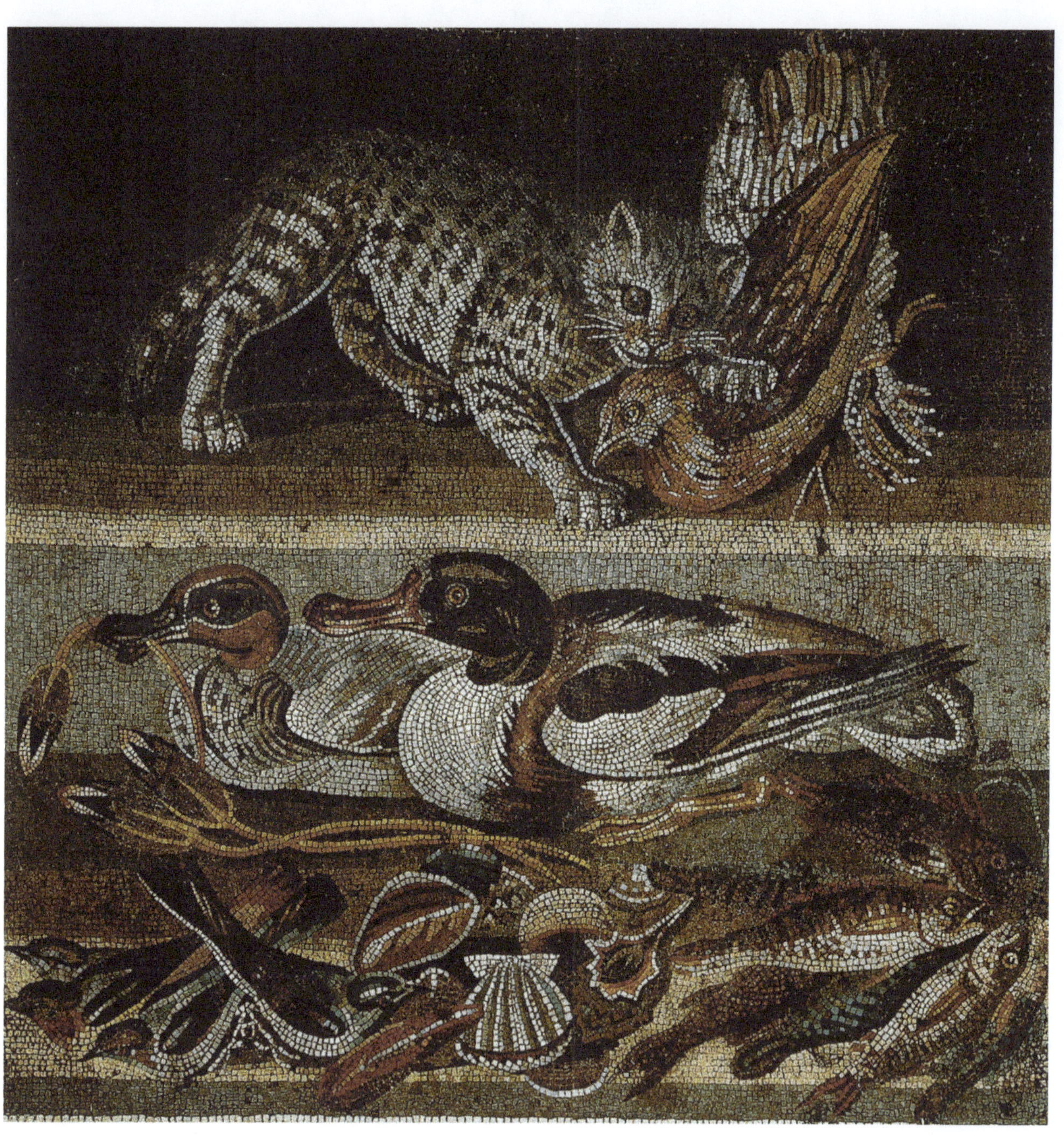

PAINTING

Sources

Practically all surviving specimens of Greco-Roman painting have been found in Campania at Pompeii or Herculaneum, and in Rome itself. These sites alone have yielded examples of ancient pictura in quantities sufficient for a reconstruction of the art, which then as now made a more direct appeal than either architecture or sculpture to the taste of the public. Owing to the perishable nature of the material and its consequent less perfect preservation, it is more difficult to study its earlier Italic stages than those of the contemporary arts. The Etruscan, the Etrusco-Latin, the Oscan schools, of all of which something has been said, developed on a Greek basis though absorbing strong Italic traits, and a school of painting seems to have flourished in Rome from the second century B.C. onward.

Character of Roman Painting — Mural Decoration

At the outset it is well to be clear as to what the Romans demanded from painting. Practically all known Roman painting is mural; this confers upon it a very special character, for being intended as wall decoration its primary function is architectural rather than pictorial. Subjects, patterns, colour are all subordinated to the divisions of the wall space, which was completely covered from floor to ceiling. This system of decoration was rendered possible by the simplicity of Roman furniture, which was of light, portable character and not intended to be placed stiffly against walls. Landscapes and figure subjects were introduced in profusion into wall painting, but always in relation to the surface to be decorated. It is worthy of note that to hang framed pictures from cords and nails as we do would have struck an ancient Greek or Roman as illogical and inorganic, and it would probably never have entered his head to destroy the unity of the wall surface in this barbarous fashion. Easel pictures existed, but they were mostly treated as panels inserted into the walls precisely as were the marble panel reliefs so much in fashion during the Empire. We hear, for instance, of small pictures inserted into the "hottest chamber" of the Baths of Agrippa, which had to be removed and repaired.

Pictures might also be framed and shuttered and placed upon shelves or ledges; an arrangement often seen imitated in wall paintings, as in Room 13 of the "Villa of the Mysteries" at Pompeii.

Classification of the Styles

The large number of Pompeian wall paintings discovered in houses that can be approximately dated with the help of a passage in Vitruvius, to a classification into four periods according to their systems of decoration. This classification, though others have from time to time been substituted in its place is so generally adopted that we retain it here for convenience. These four periods are: (1) the Incrustation style, of the second century B.C.; (2) the Architectural style, corresponding roughly to the first century, B.C. and lasting into the Julio-Claudian period; (3) the Ornate, overlapping the second style and lasting from about the middle of the principate of Augustus to the earthquake of A.D. 63; (4) the Fantastic, or Intricate, from the earthquake of 63 to the final destruction of Pompeii in A.D. 79.

The First or Incrustation Style

In the first or Incrustation style the covering of walls with white marble, or their veneering with panels of precious marble, to the exclusion of pictures, a fashion much in vogue in the Hellenistic East, was imitated in paint. The fashion of marble covering had been introduced into Rome under the Republic, when we hear of one Mamurra, a rich knight and an officer of Caesar, who decorated his house in this style. This custom of covering walls with coloured marbles was well known to the later Renascence, and the Cybo chapel at S. Maria del Popolo in Rome probably affords as good an example as any of the effect which this Pompeian style of decoration sought to produce. The so-called house of Sallust at Pompeii — shows how it was imitated in mural painting. The same style was practised likewise outside Italy as at Delos, and in Rome there is a striking example of this style in the Republican house under the *lararium* of the later Flavian Palace. As there was no room here for pictures, we may pass on to the second or architectural style into which landscape is often introduced with great effect.

The Second or Architectural Style — The Odyssey Landscapes

In this period, which extends from about the year 70 B.C. to the end of the reign of Augustus, the object is to break up the wall surface by a number of architectural features so composed as to produce the illusion of extra space. First a dark line painted along the bottom of the wall was made to appear as a continuation of the floor; above this

In this splendid detail of the Pompeian mosaic, ▶
Alexander the Great, mounted on his Bucephalus horse, assaulted the Persian king Darius III. The great Macedonian continues to be held as a model of absolute power, from the Hellenistic period to the Roman period.
Naples, National Archaeological Museum.

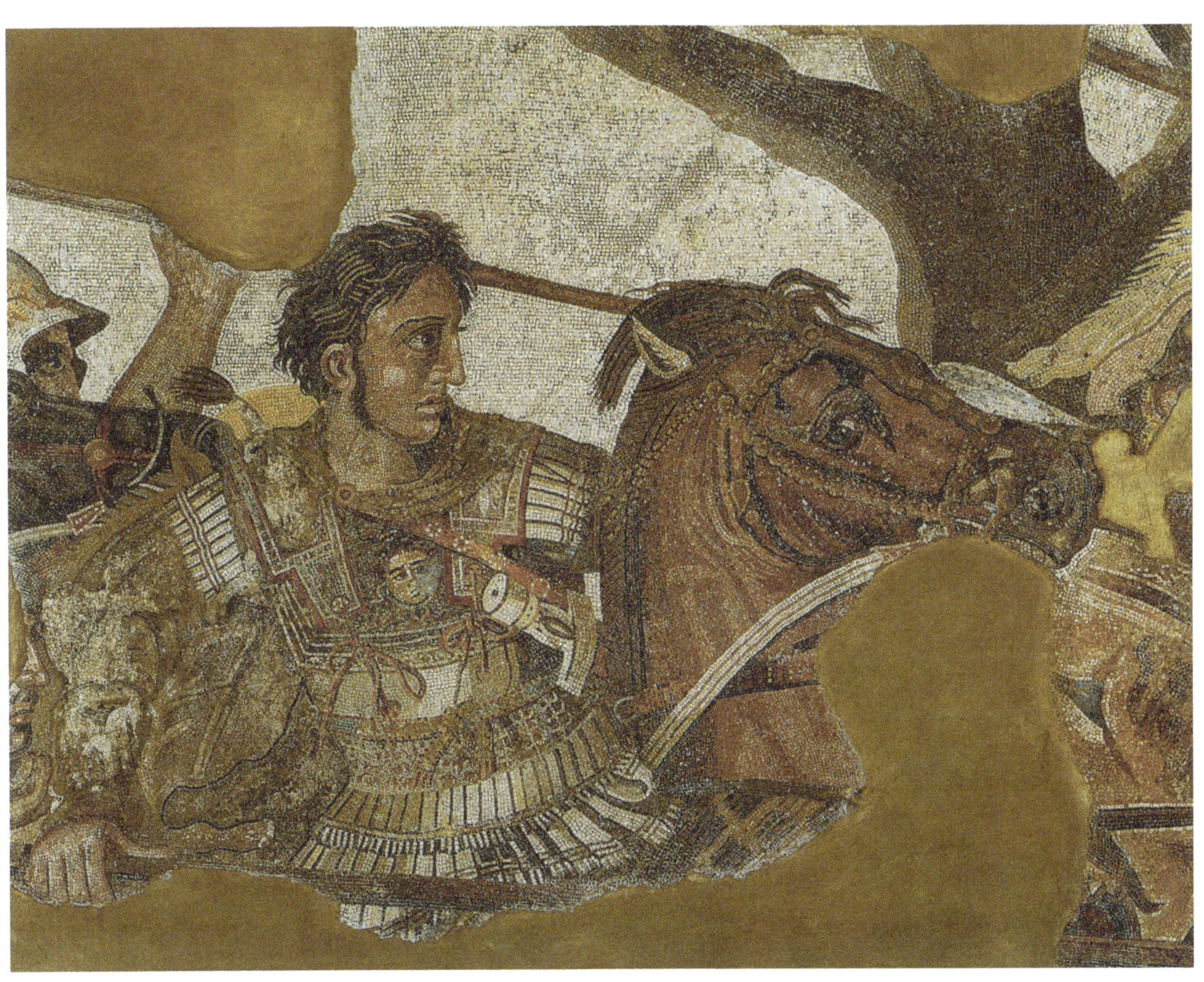

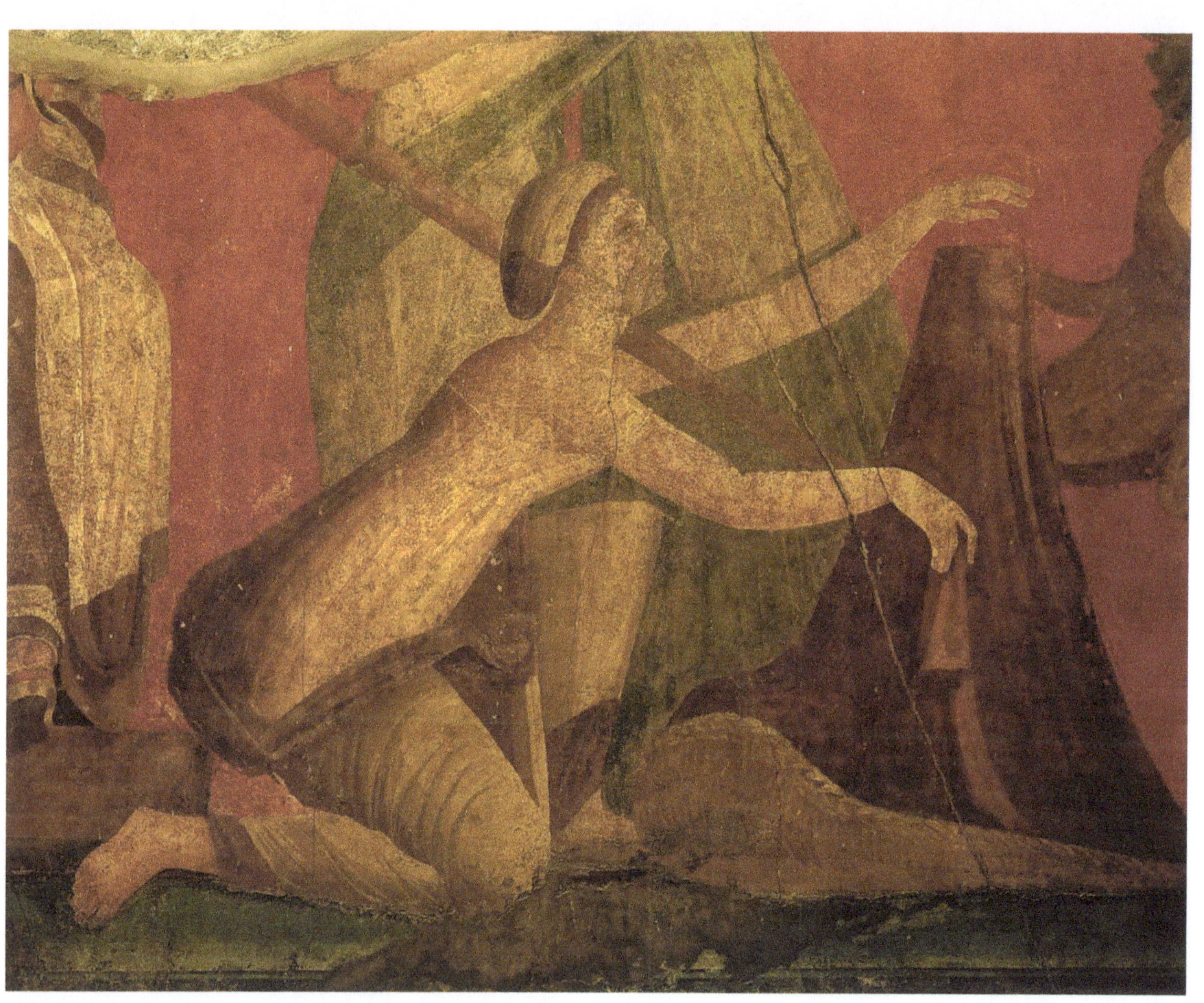

line was painted a podium or socle supporting the wall, above which ran a frieze. Openings are next imitated, first in the frieze, then in the panels, to disclose whole landscapes, enlivened more often than not by figures, and conceived of, not as panel pictures, but as representing the open country outside the wall. Sometimes the place of the frieze was taken by a simulated clerestory disclosing a continuous vista. Not infrequently columns were painted in front of the wall, standing upon the podium; the idea being to turn the room into the semblance of a cloistered court, imagined as placed within a landscape seen through the openings in the outer wall. The devices are clever for the decoration of houses in a crowded city like Rome, where land was dear and courts and gardens few, and where neighbouring houses would spring up and disagreeably block out the view. Occasionally the space left above the wall merely disclosed the sky.

One of the simplest and most beautiful mural decorations of the so-called second style is afforded by the paintings of a room belonging to a house of late Republican date discovered in the old Via Graziosa on the Esquiline, and removed to the Library of the Vatican. Here the upper part of the wall surface is treated as a clerestory, between the pilasters of which we see a continuous landscape enlivened by scenes from the Odyssey. The adventures of Odysseus among the Laestrygones

occupy three scenes, then comes the voyage to the island of Circe, followed by the central episode of the wanderer's arrival at the palace of the enchantress. These scenes are followed by others showing Odysseus at the mouth of the underworld, and the punishment of the damned. The series is now incomplete. The action of the personages is animated and lifelike; dramatic situations are piquantly seized; and a deep but simple irony, truly Homeric in its directness, takes pleasure in contrasting within one scene the panic and flight of the ships with a peaceful seascape where the sea-nymphs sun themselves on the rocks, lovely and serene as though no human tragedy had ever darkened those smiling shores.

The painter's interest in the story is proved by the inscriptions attached to the personages; yet the human feeling pales before the artist's joy in the rendering of landscape. With broad sweeps of the brush he has evoked mountain ranges, down which rush Antiphates and his men; limpid pools wherein are mirrored the watering flocks; grey-green glades and pasture lands, where dwell the shepherd Pan and the nymphs of the place; the waters of a summer sea, deepening from light green to darkest blue. In the first of the Laestrygonian pictures we see the stately figure of the daughter of the king coming to fill her pitcher in a rocky landscape; outside in a land-locked bay are the Greek ships, and above hover the wind gods. In the next picture, the grandly-drawn figure of the herdsman, seen from the back as he moves inward into the picture, is used to emphasize the depth of the landscape, just as the whole scene of Odysseus at the mouth of the

Pompeii, Villa of the mysteries, c. 60 B.C. Fresco.

underworld, where the shades rush up to lap the blood, is subordinated to the magic illumination produced by the yellow Turneresque light that falls aslant through the mouth of the cavern on to the gibbering crowd of ghosts.

The scenes may be Homeric, but they are Homer seen through modern eyes. The roles of man and of nature have been reversed, and man, no longer the central element in nature, acts as a foil to the landscapes wherein he moves. So in more modern times the Carracci and Salvator Rosa, Claude Lorrain and Gaspar Poussin peopled their landscapes with groups of figures and mythological scenes whose main function is to emphasize space values. The predominant colours used are the green, violet and yellow which appear as far back as the fourth century B.C. on the sarcophagus of Alexander from Sidon.

The so-called Third or Ornate Style — Subject Pictures

About the middle of the first century a third style of painting, known as the Composite or Ornate, made its appearance at Pompeii, which several modern critics refuse to recognize as a separate style, seeing in it only a variation on the themes of the second style. In it the old architectural divisions of socle, wall and frieze or clerestory, survive as decorative elements though they lose all functional character. The projecting lower strip and the socle alike recede into the plane of the wall. At the same time the central opening with vista in the wall surface above the socle is replaced

by an sedicula or chapel-like recess containing what is intended to imitate a panel picture; at either side the wall is divided into compartments decorated by miniature landscapes or floating figures. The empty space imagined above the wall is filled with graceful architectural details that recall certain decorations of the second style. "Reeds take the place of columns," as Vitruvius scornfully remarks, and what he calls "ribboned and streamered ornaments" are introduced, while candelabra alternate with reeds as a columnar motive. It is in this phase of the art that we first come across mythological compositions which may be compared to our own subject-pictures, kindred subjects forming pendants or a sequence being often selected for one house. For instance, in one room of the house of the "Amore Punito" we find represented on the one side Ares making love to Aphrodite, who sits pensive and unresponsive on a high-backed throne, and on the other the goddess attended by a tiny Eros full of glee that the same punishment has not been meted out to him as to his small brother, who is led away crying in disgrace by one of his mother's attendants. From another house come "Europa on the bull amid the Cretan maidens," Guida, 1296, as a pendant to "Pan piping among the nymphs," (Guida, 1298). Another pair represent "Meleager and Atalanta", and "Hercules and Dejanira with the Centaur Nessus". All these are interesting as

Samnites Warriors, 1st century B.C. ▶
Fresco from a tomb, Paestum. 112 x 199 cm. Naples,
National Archaeological Museum.

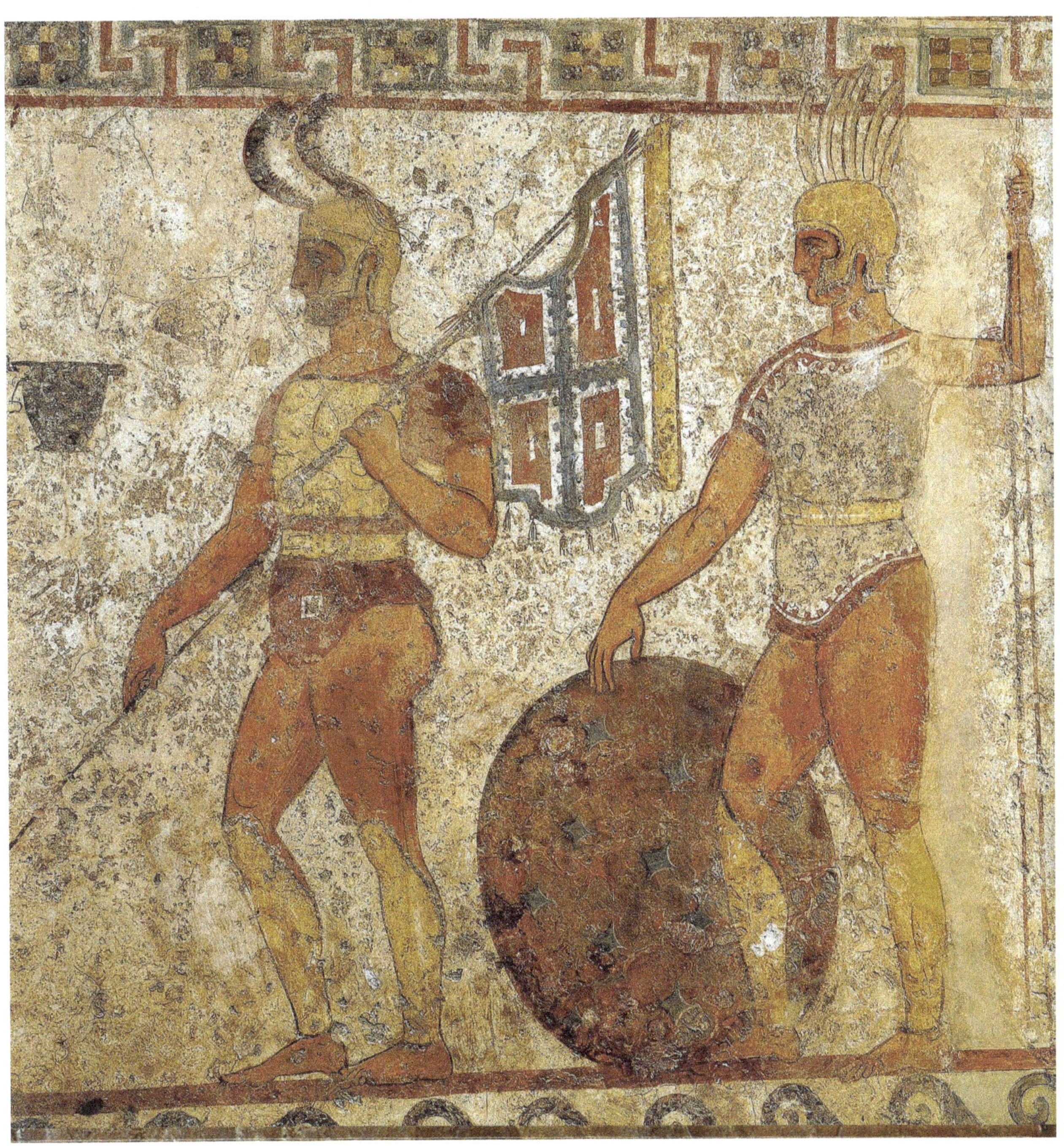

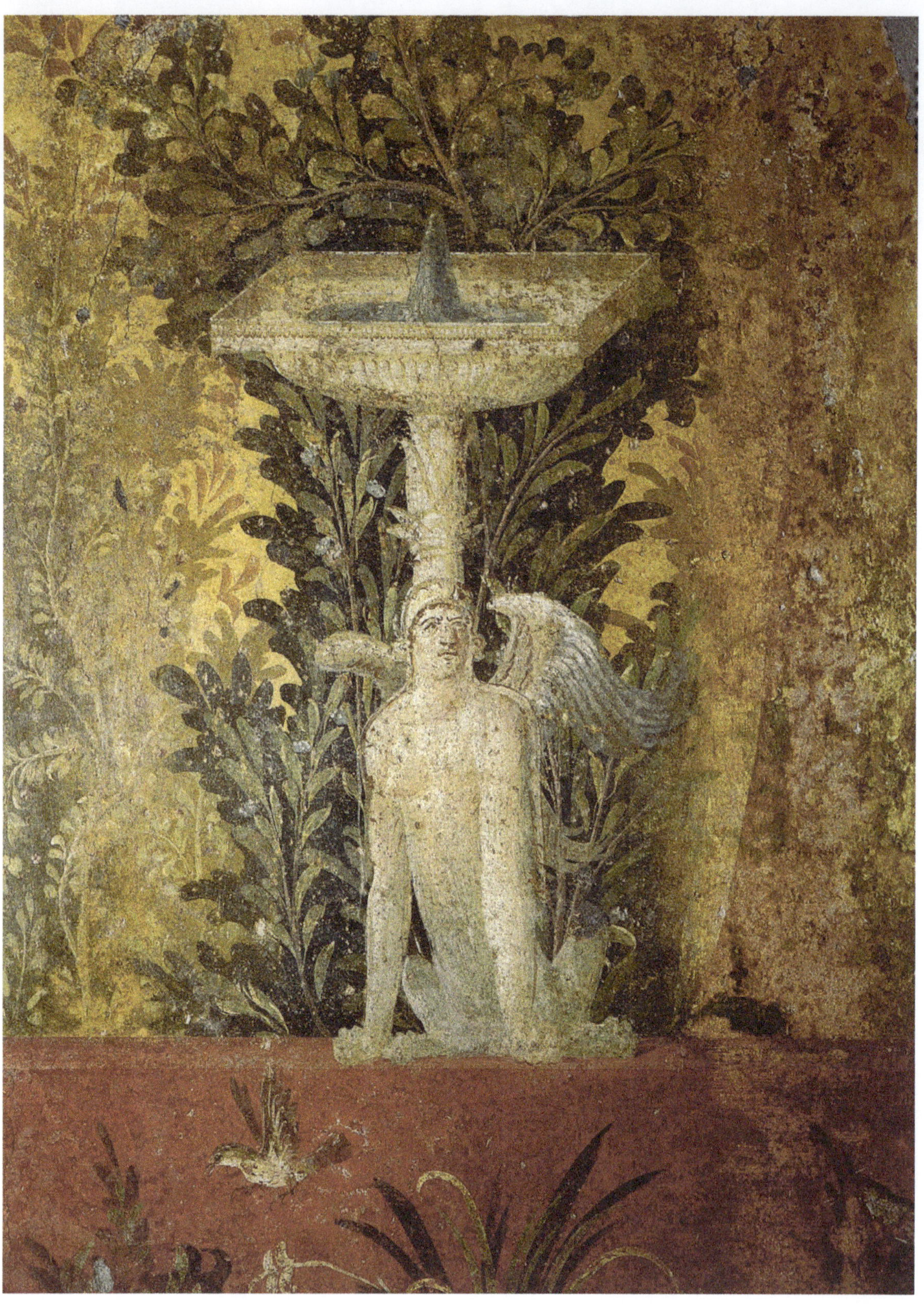

showing a new relation of figures to landscape. We have seen in the paintings of the second style the figure subordinated to the landscape; now the reaction has set in, and the landscape becomes a mere setting for the figure. So too architecture, in the "Orestes and Py lades arriving at the house of Pelias", is brought in only to serve as background to the action.

The Fourth or Intricate Style

After about A.D. 50 a fourth style of wall decoration, known as the intricate or fantastic style, made its appearance, and lasted till the final catastrophe which submerged Pompeii in A.D. 79. In reality it is only a return to the architectural schemes of the second style; and these, however fantastic, do not again lose their logical significance. The wall surface is now frequently broken up into niches decorated with painted statues, and the wall itself stands on a high ornate podium, which is not infrequently decorated, like the wall above, with figures or with pictures. The influence of stage architecture is generally claimed for this decoration, which may, however, be the simple and logical development of elements present from the first in Roman wall- painting. In this style the central space is generally reserved for the large mythological compositions, which are characteristic of the period. It is in the fourth style

likewise that landscapes with figures of pygmies, deriving, of course, from Egyptian models, begin to play so large a role, and develop into a class of landscape with buildings in the Egyptian style and Egyptian trees and plants; as in the Casa di Apolline at Pompeii, where Egyptian sycamores and palms overtop Egyptian buildings, though the figures are neither pygmies nor Egyptian, but a peasant driving his mule.

A delightful landscape in Naples shows the centre of the scene taken up by a spreading tree within an enclosure composed of three columns united by an architrave; to the right cattle graze in a meadow; in the foreground is a stream crossed by a bridge upon which we see a man with a long staff, followed by a goat; in the background are high hills, and temple-like buildings occupy the middle distance. Many equally vivid examples have been allowed to fade and even to vanish completely.

Small landscapes furnished with all the accessories of pillars, enclosures, shrines and sacred trees as in the second style also make their appearance now, while, as in the Odyssey landscapes, there is a tendency to treat the figures as mere accessories. Among favourite motives at this time are long villa facades and colonnades, glimpses of gardens and of terraces lapped by water upon which little pleasure boats are gliding. But the glory of the fourth style and what gives it special distinction is the manner in which human figures are introduced into the architecture: beneath airy pavilions Dionysus walks with the goat-legged Pan; a Maenad teases a Satyr; figures look over balustrades or "wander like sleepwalkers high up on a jutting cornice; down hanging stairways lovers advance towards one another with eager steps, and a girl may be seen balancing herself on an architrave as she plays with a sumptuous peacock.

Figure Painting of the Fourth Style

We now turn to the more formal figure painting for which the fourth style in Pompeii and Herculaneum is justly famous. A grand example from Herculaneum is the well-known picture in Naples representing the childhood of Telephus. The boy is seen on the ground on the left, nursed by the goat; above sits the local nymph, and Hercules, behind whom stands Auge, looks pensively down at the foundling he is about to adopt. The vigorous drawing, bold brushwork, and monumental composition are alike admirable. Among the innumerable pictures of this period we may cite as specially worthy of study the popular subject of "Achilles discovered by Ulysses at the court of Lycomedes"; "the boy Achilles taught by Chiron" — from Herculaneum "Bacchus visitine Ariadne"; "Hera standing before Zeus", recently reinterpreted as the meeting between the two divinities of Mount Ida — Zeus and Cybele; "Aphrodite and Adonis"; and the three famous pictures of "Medea meditating the murder of her children"; all in the Naples Gallery. Complicated spatial effects and crowded groupings are attempted at this time, as in the "Theseus and the Athenian Captives", where the huddled captives, crowding forward in eager gratitude, form a striking contrast to the calm figure of Theseus, before whom crouches a

small boy who passionately kisses the hero's feet. For purity of pose and outline, and simplicity and breadth of colouring (in spite of heavy modern retouches), nothing from the antique surpasses the lovely head, in the British Museum, of a shepherd playing on the pipes, with its almost Giorgionesque fancy and feeling. This painting is Roman and is said to have come from a columbarium of the Via Appia.

Painting, at Rome in the Period of the Fourth Style

In the period of the fourth style painting in Rome seems to have followed a somewhat different course from what it did at Pompeii. We have already referred to certain paintings from the Golden House of Nero, where further study shows the predominance of decoration in the Columbarium style. It shares with the fourth or intricate Pompeian style the love of arabesques and fantastic architectural patterns; but the pictures, though often of excellent quality and great charm, are subordinate to the general design of wall or ceiling, whereas at Pompeii large figure-subjects that occupy the principal wall-space are a significant factor in the decoration. The comparatively small pictures of the Roman

Pompei. House of Fauna, triclinium of the main atrium ▶
detail of the Emblema in opus Vermiculatum:
A feline is overlapped by a Dionysian demon.
Naples, National Archaeological Museum.

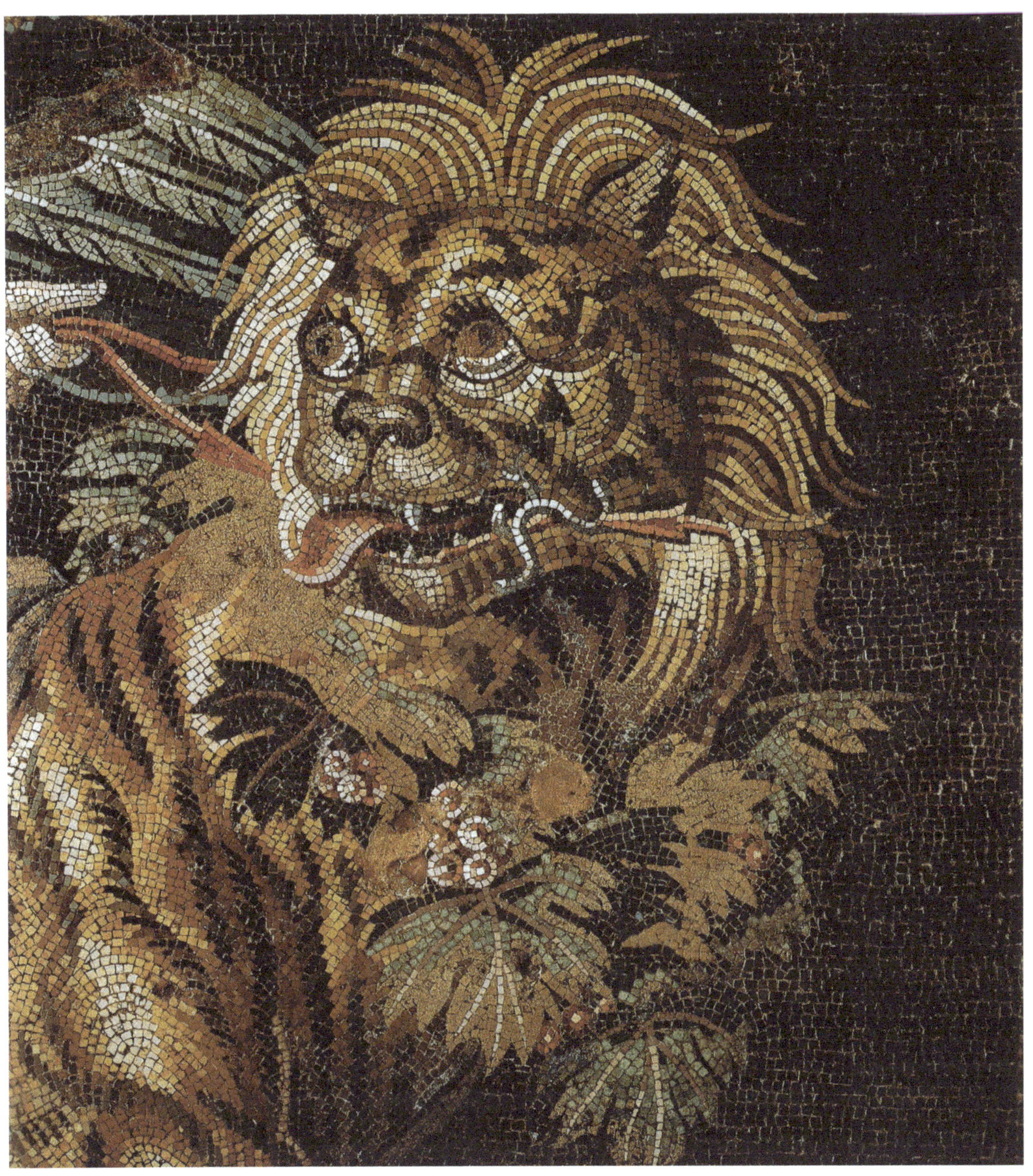

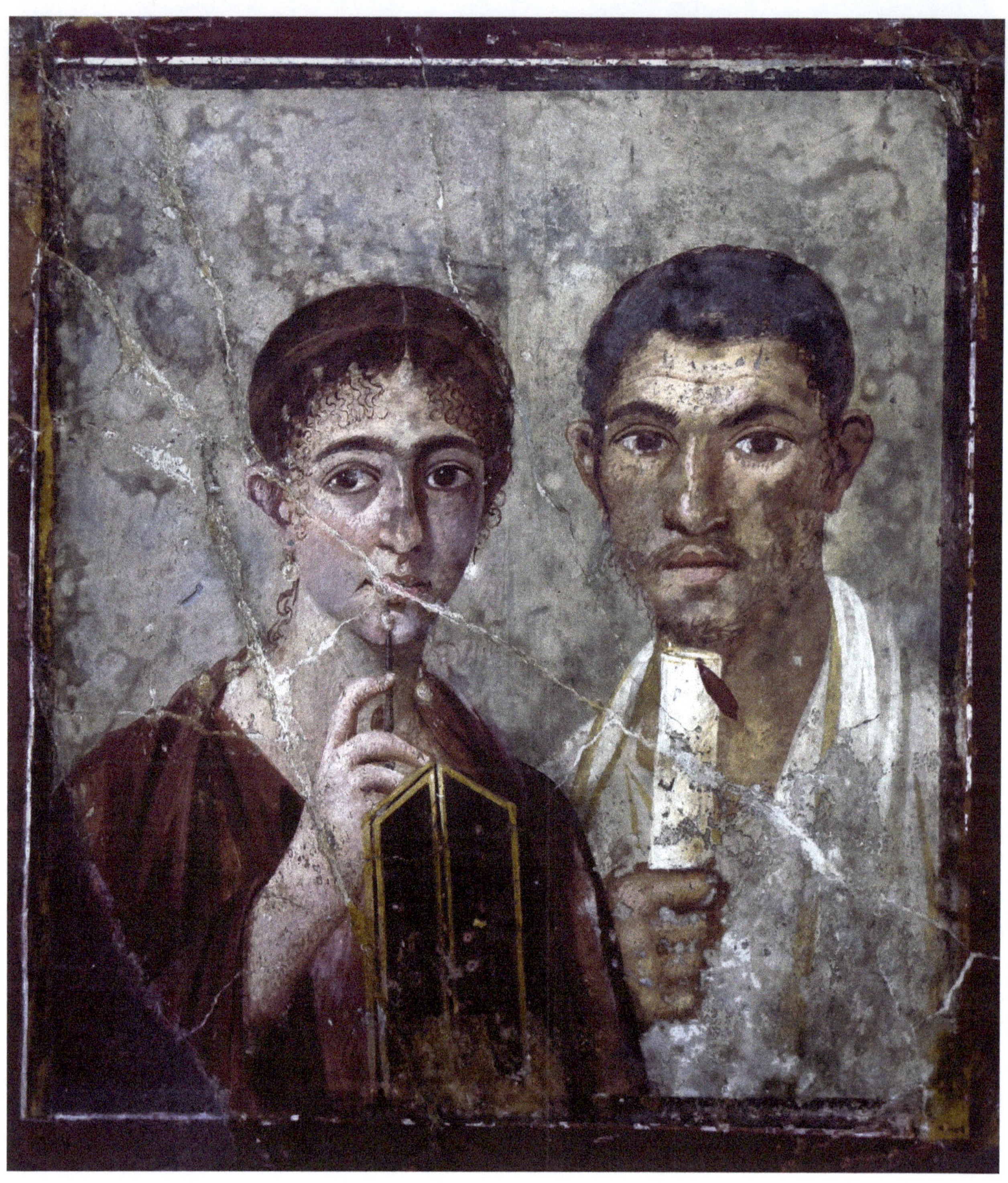

fourth style, when placed at a great height, show a charmingly patterned ceiling with fantastic animals within foliated squares.

A number of delightful wall paintings have been discovered by A. Munoz in his excavations of the Golden House. In Room 80, known as that of the Laocoon, remarkable paintings were recovered in Dr. Weege's excavations of 1912. They apparently formed part of a Trojan cycle including "Hector's Parting from Andromache" (amusingly misinterpreted by older draughtsmen as Coriolanus and his mother), so that we shall probably be correct in looking upon this room as the one in which Nero recited his " Taking of Troy ". The name of one of the painters employed on the Golden House — they must have been legion — has been preserved by Pliny . He was one Famulus, "grave and severe in his person', who worked "always wearing the toga, even when mounted on the scaffolding" — which may only mean that the cumbersome garment marked him out as the padrone of a large gang of assistants. Pliny, who rather foolishly called' the Golden House "the prison of his art," also notes a Minervava by him, " whose eyes are turned to the spectator from whatever side he may be looking." Colour laid on to flat surfaces did not satisfy the luxuriant tastes of the Neronian epoch. Gilt stucco ornaments came into fashion, as in the room of the Golden

House known as the Volta Dorata. But it does not appear that actual subject-compositions in stucco were at any time painted or gilded.

Other paintings, a little earlier perhaps than those of the Domus Aurea, are in a house of Julio-Claudian date on the Palatine, afterwards buried under the Flavian palace. Next to an exquisite nymphaeum adorned with clusters of slender columns is a room whose pavement and walls are incrusted with marble, while a decoration, including a series of little pictures from the Trojan cycle carried out partly in stucco and partly in paint, is let into the ceiling.^ But all this, like everything found of recent years on the Palatine, is unpublished. With Julio-Claudian paintings must also be reckoned the delicate wall decorations, including putti, recently removed to the Terme from the Galleria Rospigliosi, which had formerly adorned a house under the Rospigliosi Palace.

From Ostia come two scenes composed as pendants, so Augustan in spirit that it seems reasonable to assign them to his principate. On the one, a group of children — from the dress all of them boys — are forming in the procession on the right, while another group, torches in hand, are singing a hymn to the potens Diana of the Carmen Saeculare. On the second picture two boys, veiled and crowned as priests, are engaged in a ritual scene; on the right a child carries a banner; on the left a ritual ship is being dragged to shore by two more boys. These mural paintings have long been in the Museo Profano of the Vatican. Or they may be figuring as the bride and bridegroom of a ritual marriage.

Portraiture in Painting

It is only lately that any attention has been paid to the ancient painted portraits, which must have been as common as the portrait bust. The Mosaic of Virgil, copied in the second century from an original of the first proves that portrait painting was practised from an early date. The vogue must have increased, since in the last century of the Republic Varro had collected, it is said, as many as seven hundred miniature portraits of illustrious men which he inserted into his writing. He presumably found much material in the public libraries, where statues or more probably busts of authors were placed over the cases which contained their writings.

Already under the Republic a certain maiden lady whose name is variously given as Jaja or Laia of Cyzicus, painted, according to Varro, with the cestrum on ivory, portraits of women, and, moreover, by the help of the looking-glass (at/ speculum), painted a likeness of herself. Some echo of this portrait may have survived in the charming head from Pompeii of a girl with a pencil against her lips, popularly known as a poetess. Claudius thought to please the people by substituting the face of Augustus for that of Alexander on the picture of the Macedonian king which Augustus himself had placed in his Forum. Under Nero we hear of one Terentius of Lucania, a portrait painter, who executed for a portico at Antium a number of heads of gladiators and other servitors, a series that reminds us of the portraits of charioteers in the Terme; a later instance of the fashion has survived in the large mosaic with gladiators now in the Lateran which was found in the Baths of Caracalla.

Nero himself was painted on a canvas of colossal scale for a room of the palace of the Lamian Gardens on the Esquiline, but so perishable is painting that no traces of any of these works have survived. On Italian soil, it is only at Pompeii that we have undoubted examples of ancient portrait-painting, and these might be more numerous had we not, unmindful of many warnings, allowed the mass of medallion portraits discovered there to perish. A number of these may be studied in Paris, at the Ecole des Beaux-Arts, in the watercolour copies by M. Gusman, who has, moreover, reproduced not a few in his book on Pompeii. The majority belong to the later or Augustan phase of the second or architectural style, which lasted into the Julio-Claudian period. Thanks to its removal to Naples, the double portrait of Terentius Neo and his wife has been admirably preserved. Another, first published in the Archaeological Journal, is of a little boy of the Augustan age. It has now vanished.

Every one must be struck by the close likeness of those Pompeian examples to the earlier of the portraits painted on wood panels which,

An athlete of the series who adorned the mosaic ▶
pavement of one of the lateral exedras of the baths
of Caracalla. Athletes have always enjoyed great
consideration in antiquity and the athletes themselves were
widely popular with the public who frequented the thermal
baths. Rome, Vatican Museum.

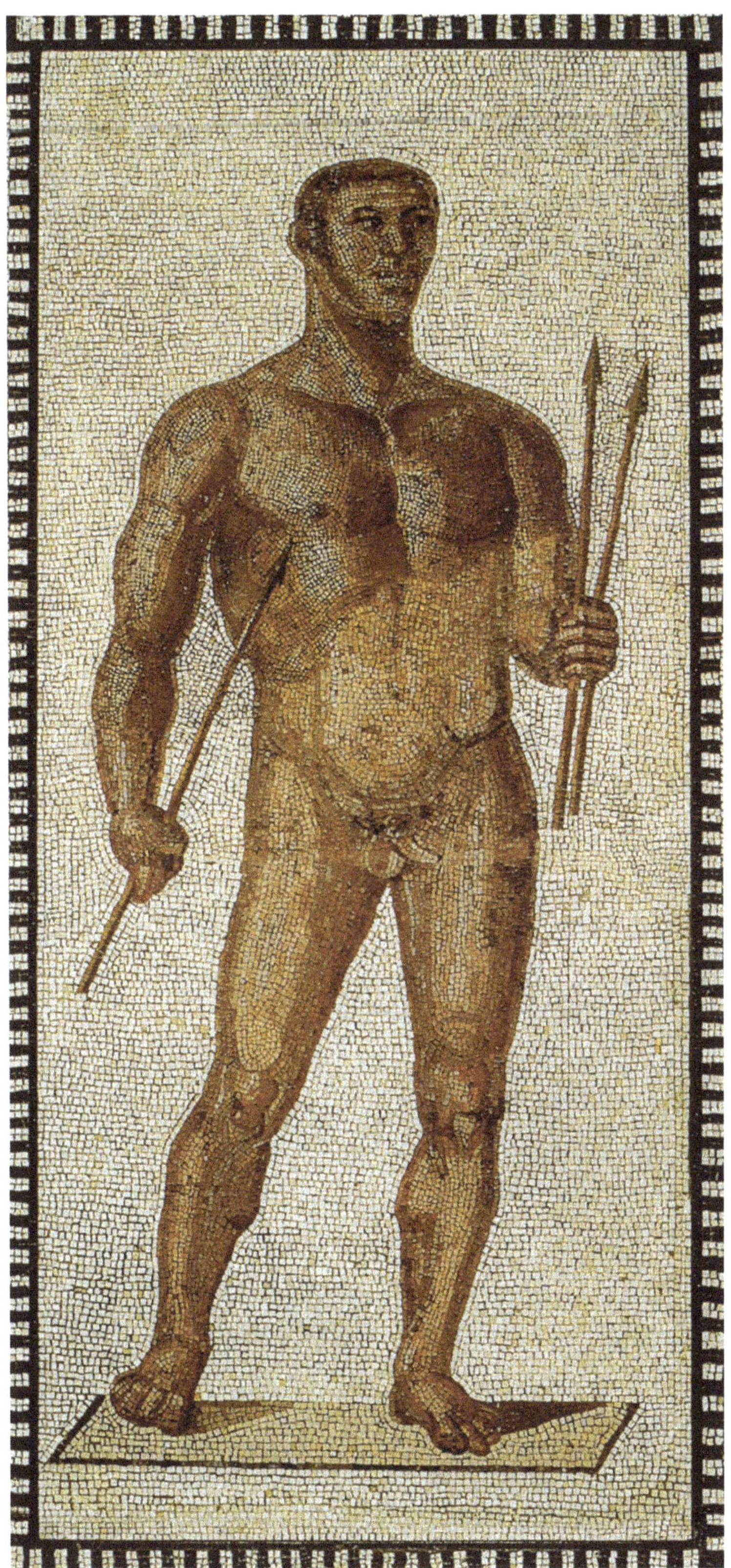

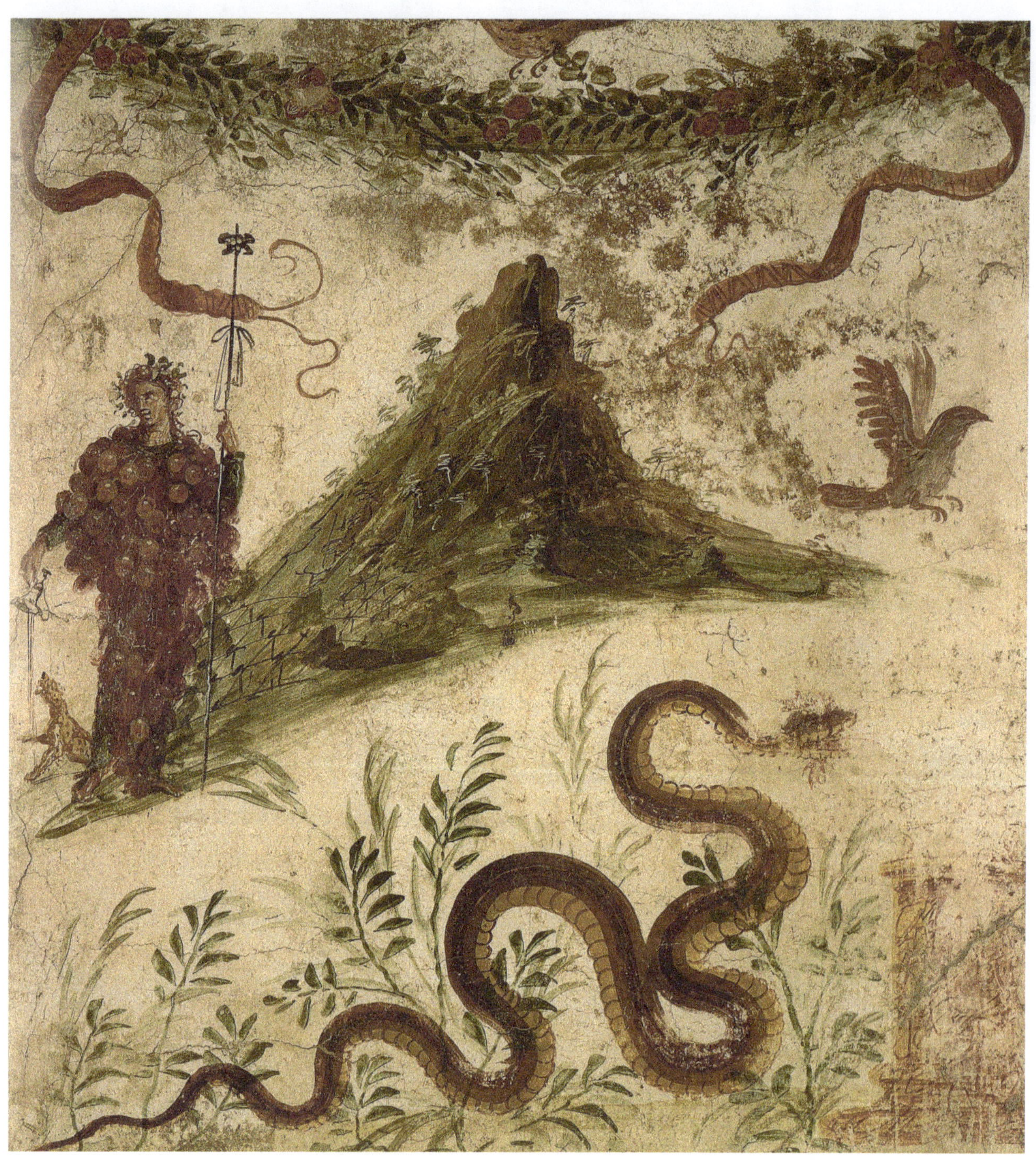

from the end of the Ptolemaic period to the period of Septimius Severus onward, were let into the mummy case and have been found in quantities in the Fayoun. This confirms the supposition that influences flowing from Egypt to Italy in the first century affected the whole Roman portraiture.

Mosaic from the last century of the Republic to the Julio-Claudian period — Transcripts of Painting — opus sectile

Closely allied to painting are the mosaic pictures, which in reality are a kind of painting with the added advantages of permanence, and of a brilliancy of colouring unknown to other processes. These pictures are invariably carried out in opus Vermiculatum ; that is, the tesserae are cut into various shapes and sizes so that every line of the design, however curved and twisted, can be followed as faithfully as with the brush and paint. This style of mosaic probably made its way fully developed into Italy from Egypt, about the close of the second or beginning of the first century.

Roman soil has so far yielded no pieces of earlier date; but we have a grand example of the early

◄ *Bacchus and Vesuvius*, 68-69 A.D. Fresco of the atrium of the Centennial House, 140 x 102 cm.
Naples, National Archaeologica Museum.

part of the first century at Palestrina, in a mosaic which may, as we have seen, be the very one presented by Sulla to the oracular cave of the shrine of the Fortuna of Praeneste. We may describe it here at somewhat greater length as it is the first of an important series. The admirable design, in which something higher has surely been attained than a mere "learned dissertation upon fish", shows a number of fish of various kinds darting backwards and forwards through the water with lively movements. Possibly the illusion was rendered more intense by covering the mosaic at times with a shallow sheet of water shows the forepart of a fish as he swims towards a pillar dedicated to Poseidon. It reminds one of Strabo's description of the shrines of Poseidon on the headlands by the sea.

The pillar, tied with a sash or fillet, stands within the typical enclosure; and in front of it burns an altar raised on two steps and adorned with garlands. The strong and vivid colouring is carried out in only four shades — yellow, brown, red and purple. Fish mosaics, that is, mosaics imitating fish swimming in tanks, became very fashionable in the late Republic and under the Empire. They were intended to represent in a permanent form the fish ponds of which we find traces all over Italy, both in the interior and along the seashore. One admirable example from Pompeii, well known as the "Battle of the Fish," represents an octopus seizing his enemy the lobster, while a number of other fish swim terrified in all directions. A religious significance probably attached to these representations and accounts for their popularity.

There seems no reason for dating the large and famous "Barberini mosaic" of Palestrina, which was found in the apse of the shrine of Fortuna, either in Hadrianic or Augustan times.

The purely Egyptian subject, life on the banks of the Nile, is in harmony with the intrusion of Egyptian fashions in later Republican times. The illustration chosen gives one of its most important scenes, with Roman soldiers feasting under the awning in front of a pavilion on the banks of the Nile, while all around are the various details of a conventional Nile landscape. Interesting transcripts of pictures are found among Pompeian mosaics. One of the most famous is the "Battle of Alexander and Darius" in the Naples Museum — after a famous picture by the Graeco-Egyptian painter Helena, that hung at a later date in Vespasian's "Forum of Peace".

Two others which are composed as pendants, remind us in the choice of their subjects — a group of strolling players, and two young ladies consulting a sorceress — of the little triptychs in the House of Augustus and the House of the Farnesina. But in this case the figures are masked, and thus betray their direct derivation from scenes of the Attic Middle Comedy. On the dark strips at the bottom of the mosaic of the strolling players we read the name Dioscorides of Samos. A fourth mosaic, of which two slightly different versions exist, the one found near Pompeii, the other in the Villa Albani, found at Sarsina, introduces us to an assembly of the Seven Sages, who sit pleasantly conversing outside a pillared enclosure that resembles the sacred precincts on certain landscapes of the architectural style.

The finished composition of these mosaics, and the fact that the signatures, when we have any, are Greek, make it probable that here, as in the case of the "Hellenistic" reliefs or the wall paintings, we have Greek artists working for Roman and Italian patrons. Besides the Dioscorides mentioned above, we find the signature of the Greek Herakleitos on a large mosaic in the Lateran which represents, evidently in direct imitation of the mosaic by Sosus of Pergamon described by Pliny, an unswept floor where mice are making off with the scraps of food that have fallen from the table. Be it noted, by the way, that not Romans, but refined Graeco-Asiatics invented and took delight in the unsavoury subject.

Possibly the whole has a religious meaning that now escapes us. This seems indicated by the presence of the stork, the duck, the fish, and the statuettes of divinities in other parts of the border. In the collection of mosaics at Naples, we find mythological subjects such as Theseus and the Minotaur, or the punishment of Lycurgus; and numerous scenes from animal life, ranging from the cock-fight to the celebrated dog inscribed Cave Canem. A mosaic of exceptional beauty represents the triumph of "Autumn," imaged as a nude winged boy, ivy-crowned and riding a panther with a wreath of poplar-leaves round his neck.

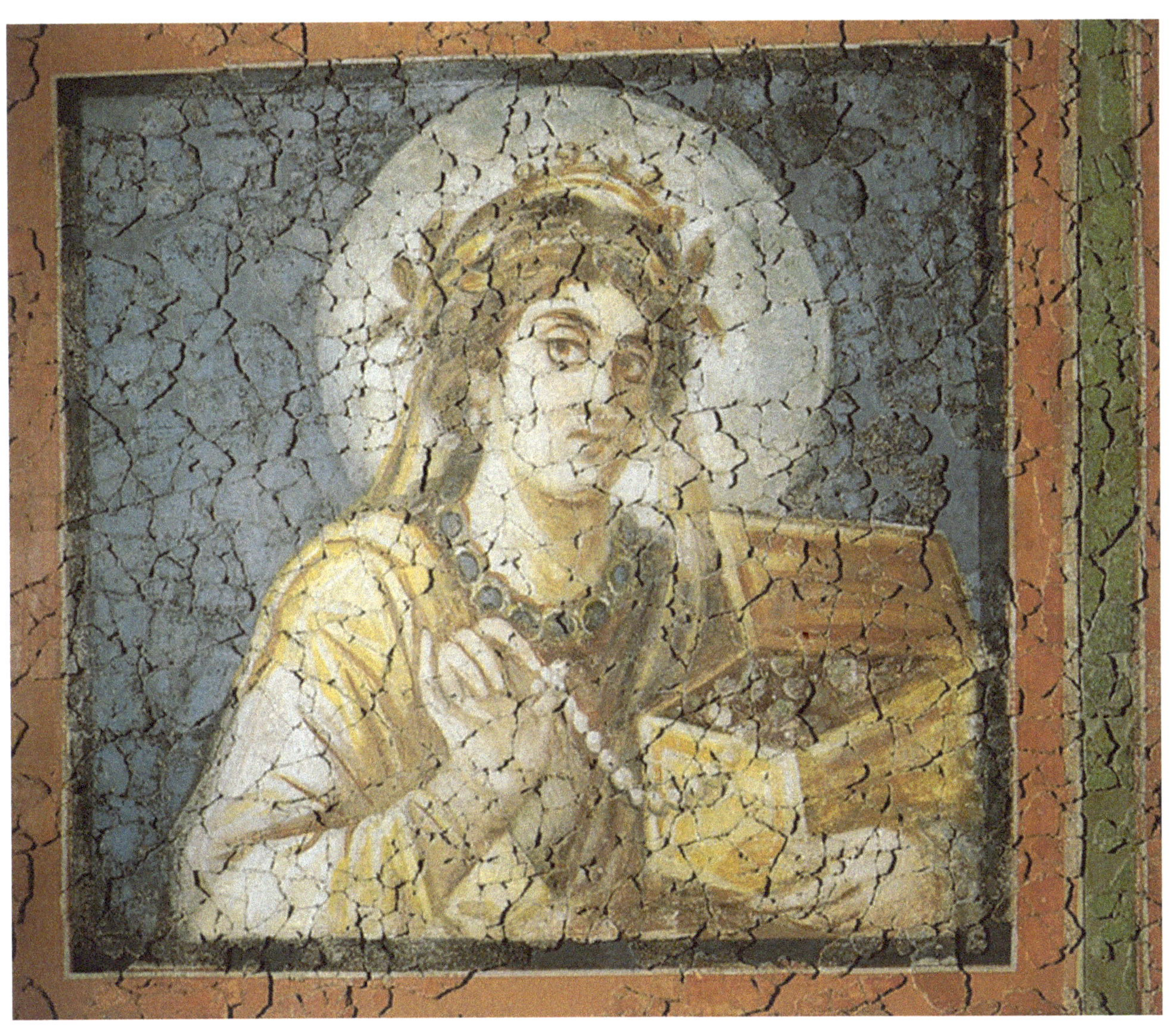

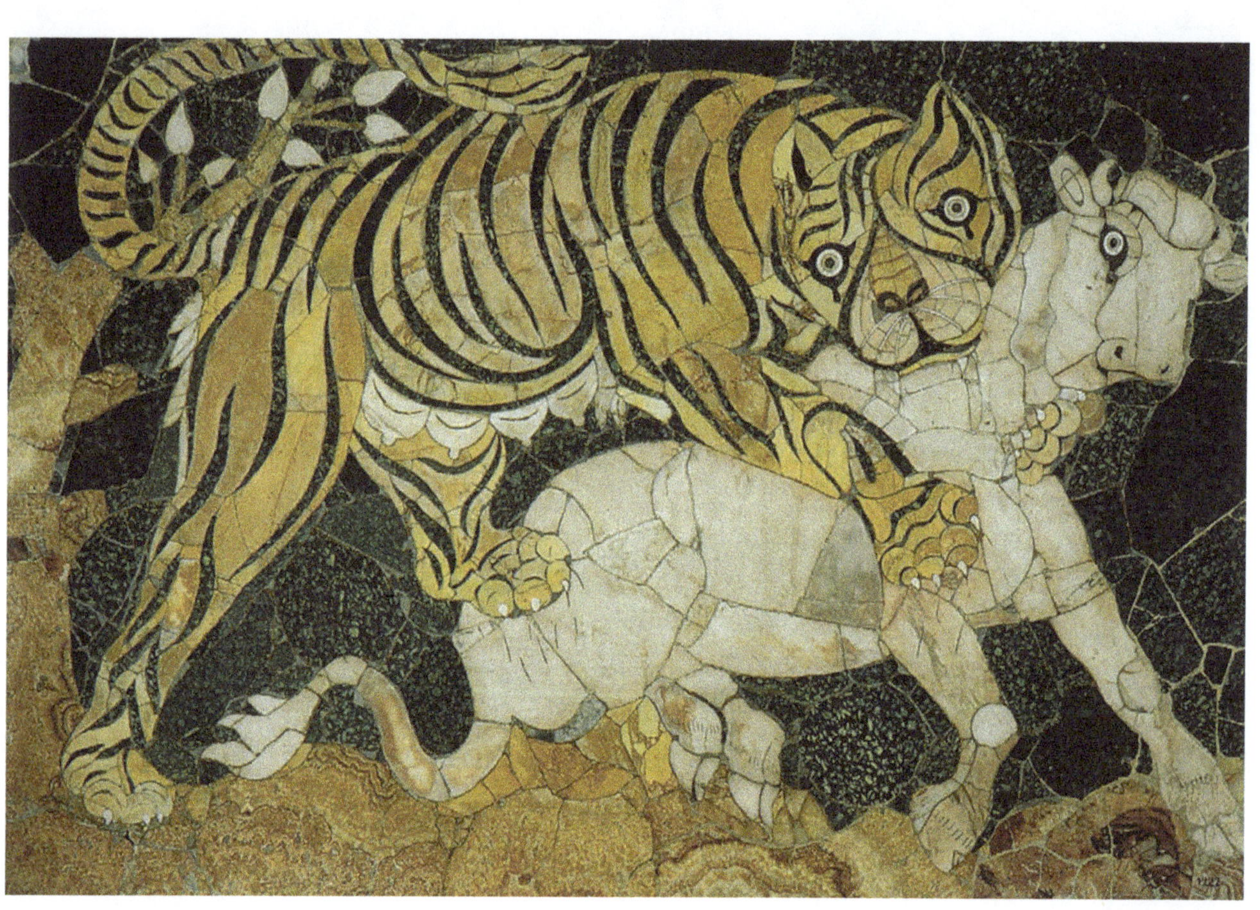

Egyptian landscapes long continued in fashion. They often reproduce scenes on the Nile, like the frieze in Naples which once framed the mosaic of Alexander from the House of the Faun at Pompeii, or the large square mosaic from the Aventine in the Museo delle Terme, where pygmies are attacking a crocodile and a hippopotamus on the banks of the Nile. The attempt at expressing depth and the fusion of the different features of the scene show a great advance on the simple disconnected composition of the Palestrina mosaic. Opus sedile, a marble intarsia or marquetry, was much in fashion. A good example of Augustan date is in the collection of Prince Colonna in Rome. It represents the childhood of Romulus and Remus, who are being suckled by the wolf in the presence of Roma and of the shepherd Faustulus; the colours employed are white and yellow for the figures, and black for the ground.

Decorated pavements — opus signinum and opus tessellatum : early pavements of Forum and Palatine

The coarse and simple mosaic known as opus signinum, because it was supposed to have been first used at Signia, appears to be of considerable antiquity; it is merely a pavement of pounded tiles and chalk into which rude geometrical designs formed by pebbles were inserted. A third variety, opus tessellatum, is composed of small equal-sized cubes of marble set in straight lines, or patterns formed of combinations of straight lines, into a bed of cement; the numerous black-and-white mosaics used for the decoration of pavements are carried out in this technique. The mosaic of a Republican or early imperial house on the Palatine is described as follows in Signor Bonis report.

"The threshold and the pavement are in slabs of the most beautiful and precious African red breccia, separated by slabs of green- veined cipollino marble from the island of Eubcea." The atrium, he continues, and the lateral rooms or cubicula "are paved with marble slabs which covered mosaic floors belonging to an earlier period. These mosaics are not composed of fragments of marble, but of pebbles from the Umbrian confluents of the Tiber, red, yellow, green and black limestone, grouped so as to produce a polychromatic effect, which is not only beautiful in itself, but also interesting as important evidence of that inspiration towards a kind of decoration the taste for which the Romans were able to satisfy to the utmost later on, when they came in contact with the Eastern and African marbles."

An interesting example of Republican floor mosaic may be seen in the pavement of the temple of the Castores below the level of the bases of the columns of the Imperial restoration of A.D. 6; and similar mosaics may be studied in the House

◀ *Animal fight*. Rome, "Basilica" of Junius Bassi, c. 331 Apr. J. Wall decor in opus sectile with marbel in color. Rome, Palazzo dei Conservatori.

of Augustus on the Palatine, and in the Domus Pontificia, or House of the Pontifex Maximus near the temple of Vesta, where also are faint traces of Republican paintings. The line mosaic pavements, with black lineo-floral ornament on white ground, of the hypogeum near the Porta Maggiore, also deserve mention.

Origins of the Roman Subject Picture

We cannot touch here on the difficult question whether the Roman and Pompeian wall paintings and mosaics which reproduce subject-pictures were or were not copied from Greek or Alexandrian models. The balance of evidence seems to be rather in favour of assuming the influence of such models, and doubtless the copying of single figures, and the copying and adaptation of groups; yet of allowing the Italian wall-decorators the merit of having exercised great discretion, and even taste in readapting these models to the actual surroundings to be decorated. It has been well noted, for instance, that in the House of the Vettii the lights in the large pictures of the triclinium are expressly adapted to harmonize with the conditions of lighting of the room.

One other point calls for mention. Recently various scholars have put forward the attractive theory that in certain cases at least, illustrated manuscripts served the Roman and Pompeian painters as models. The Homeric scenes in the "House of the Cryptoporticus " at Pompeii may be a case in point, and possibly the Homeric series

in the Julio-Claudian house on the Palatine had a like origin. We might conjecture the same for the Odyssey landscapes of the Via Graziosa in the Vatican Library. The early existence of parchments with illustrations of Trojan episodes seems proved by a manuscript of Virgil, No. 3225 in the Vatican Library, which, though itself of fourth-century date, reproduces the typical landscapes and little shrines in the second Pompeian style. And we have already alluded, in connection with the mosaic of Virgil, to the portrait of the poet at the beginning of a manuscript of his works which was seen by Martial.

Figure of a pugiliste, a mosaic from the Baths of Caracalla ▶
In addition to the rooms for the various baths, the spa facilities included palestres for physical exercise, libraries, relaxation and conversation rooms. Vatican Museum.

▼ *Overview of the great Dionysian fresco* of the luxurious triclinium of the Villa of Mysteries, unearthed in 1929-1930 under the direction of Amedeo Maiuri.

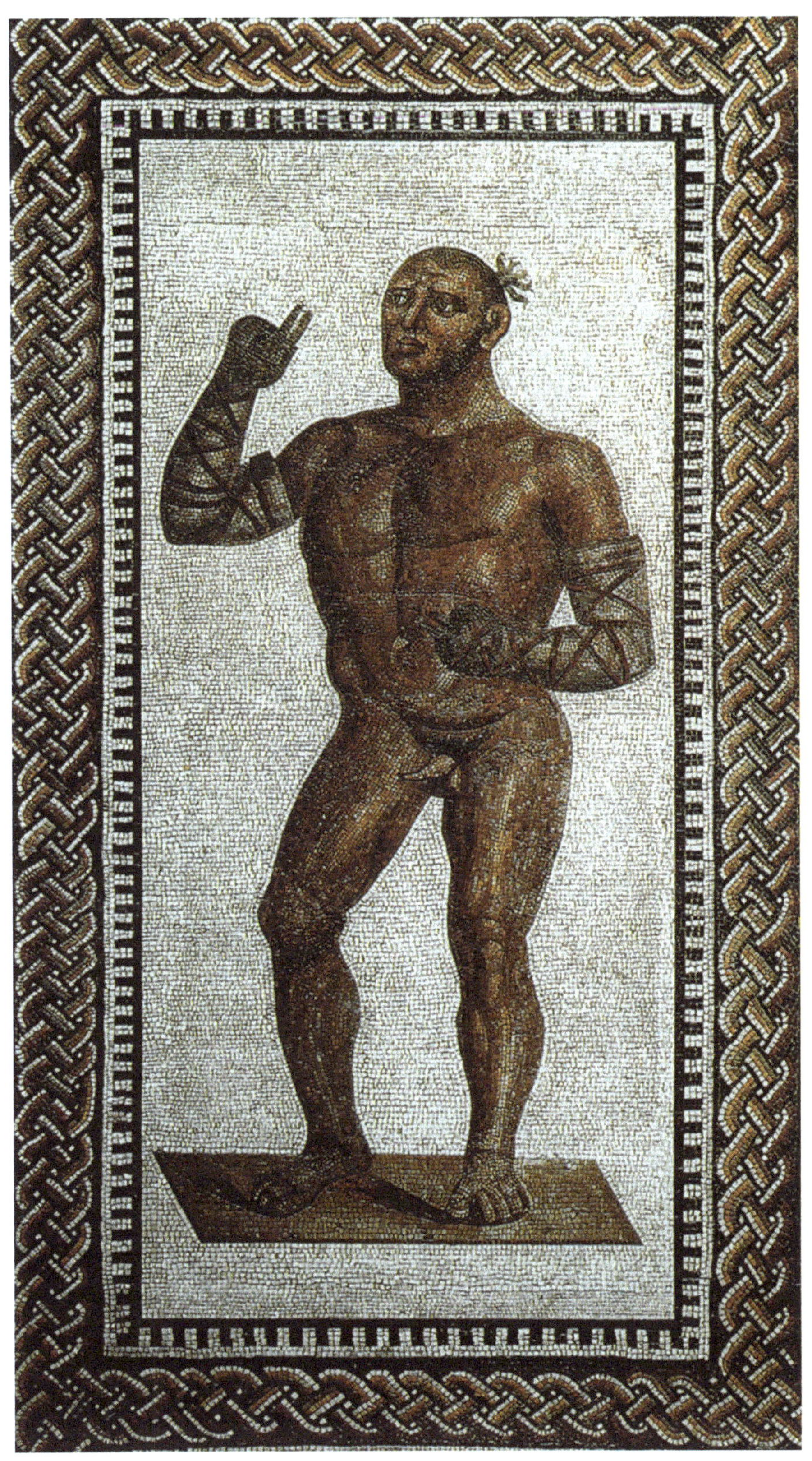

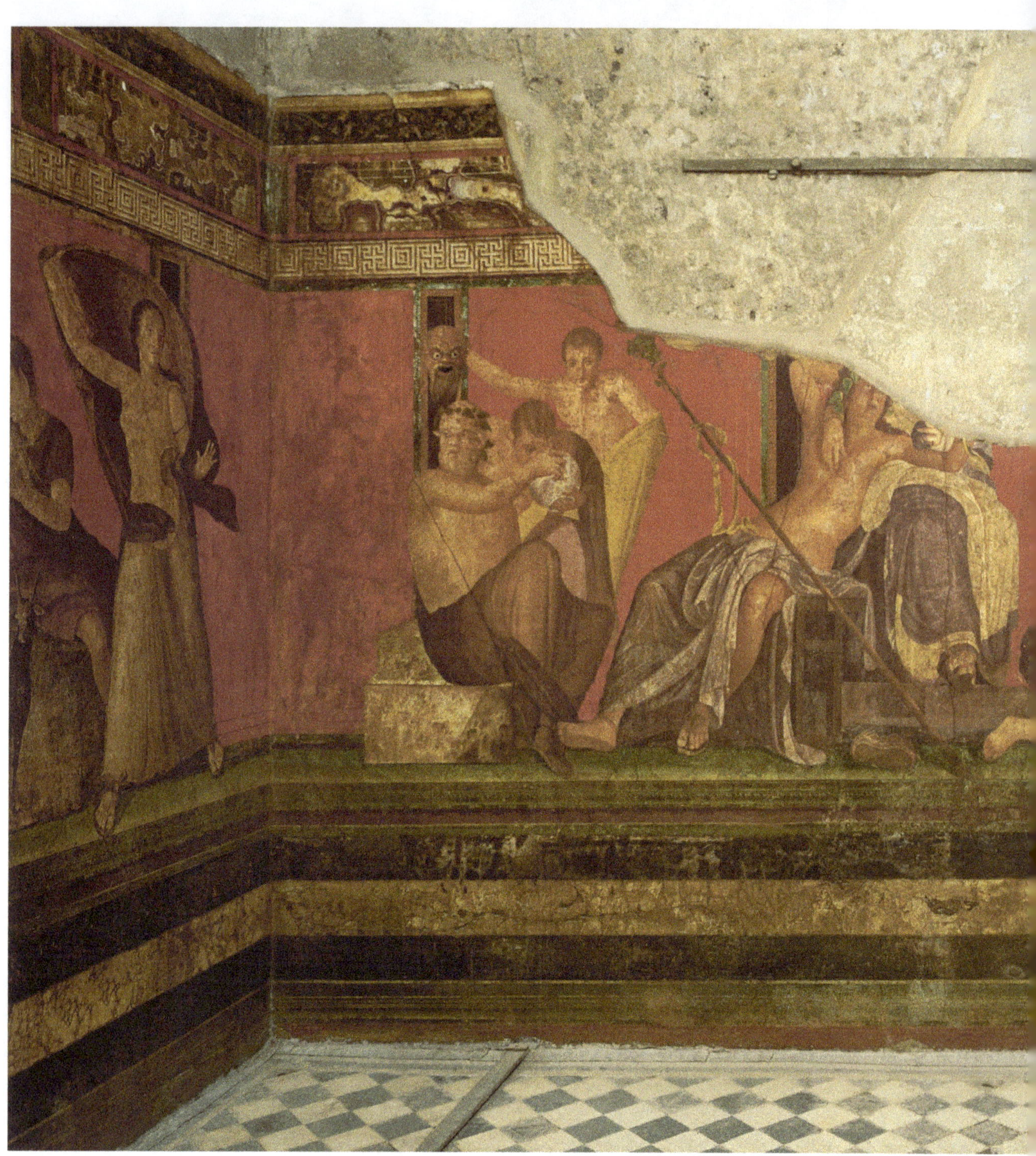

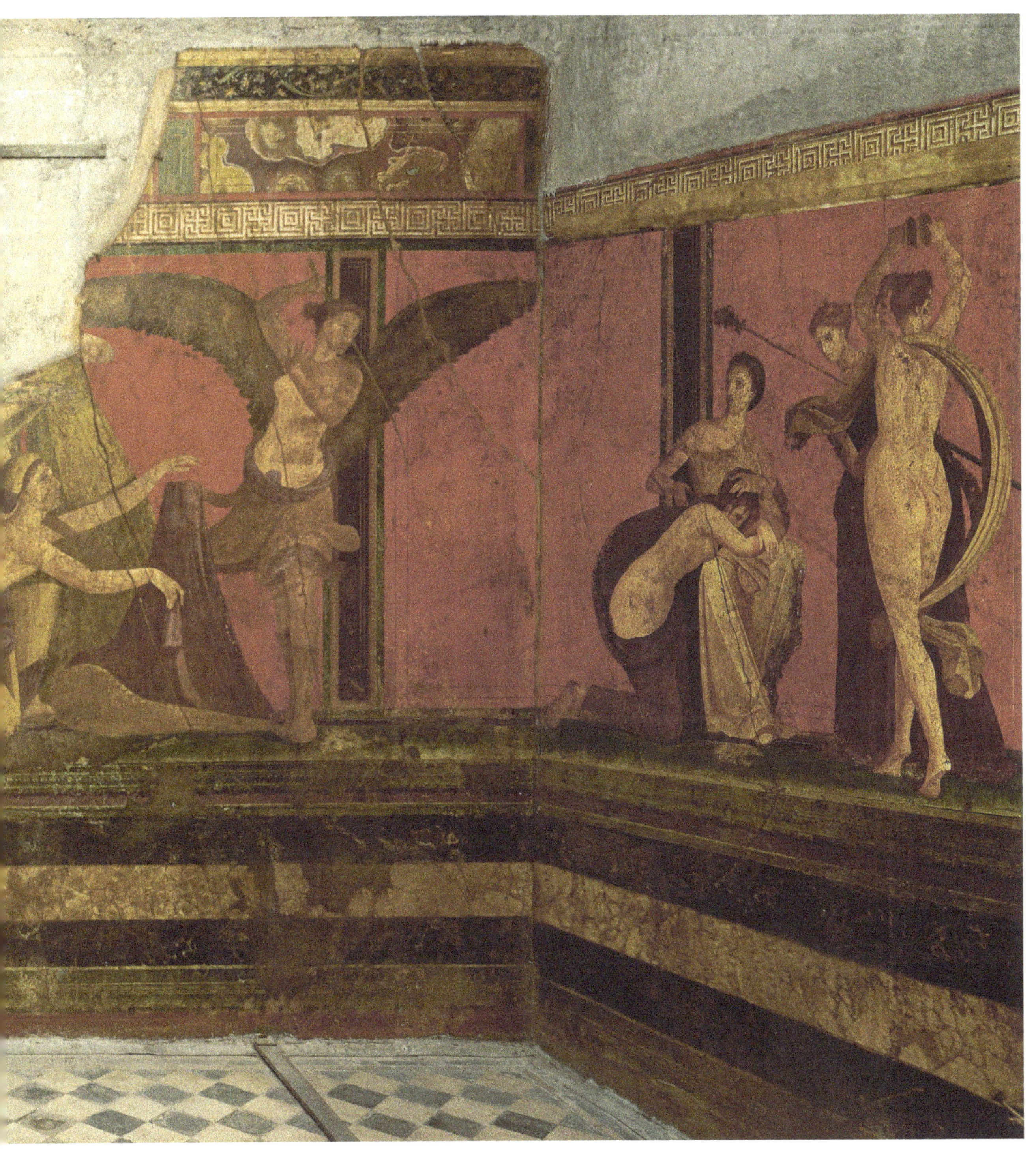

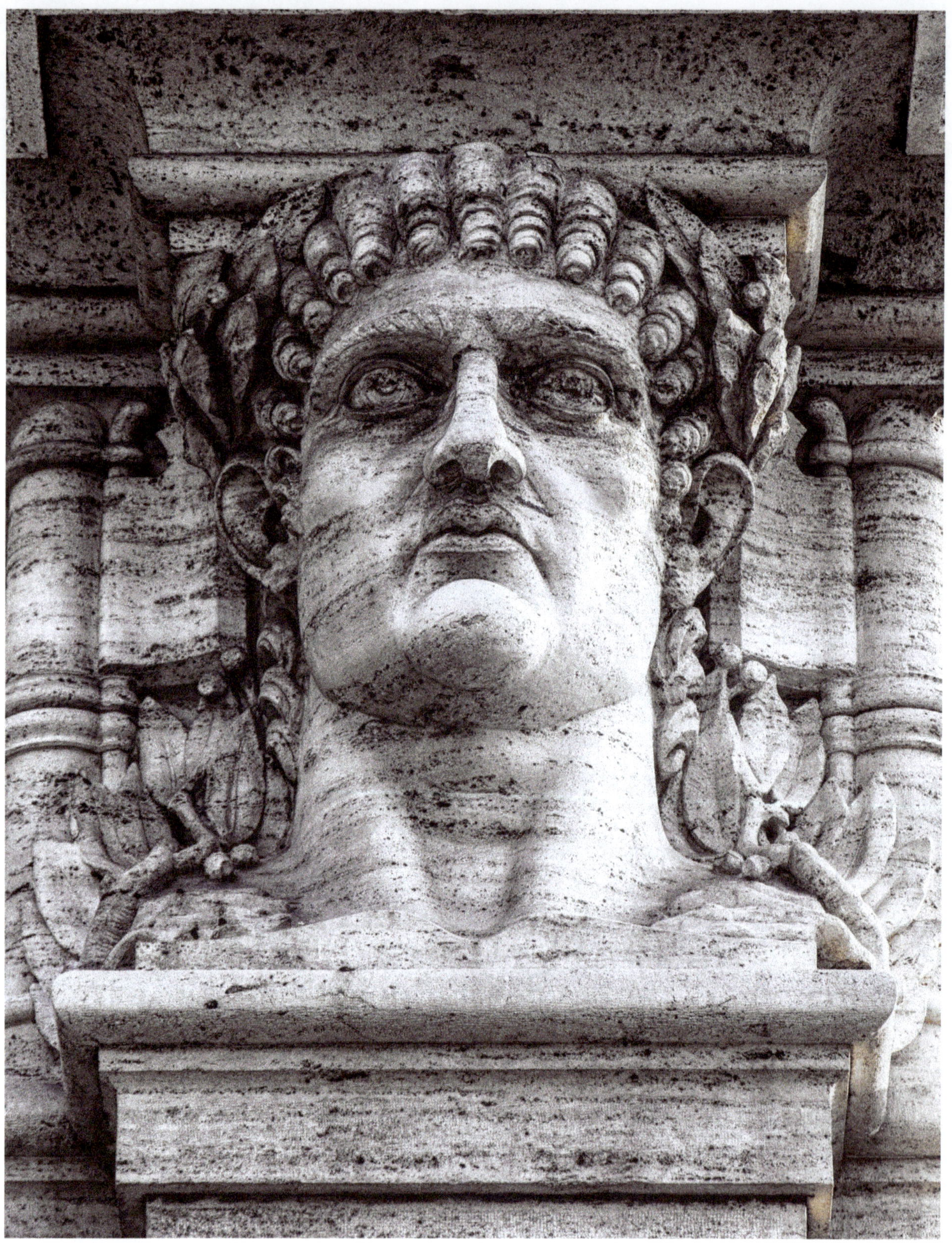

SCULPTURE

The Etruscan, from the sixth century onward, not only brings to Rome his religion and his science of augury, he digs the sewers, builds the temples, erects the first statues; he forges the arms by which Rome is to reduce him to subjection. He casts bronze, and his bronzes, in which he reveals his genius for uncompromising expression, have a bitter force that is as rugged and hard as the oak clumps of the Apennines. The symbol of Rome, the rough she- wolf of the Capitol, was made by an old Tuscan bronze worker.

As to the Roman statue maker, his work is to manufacture for the collector innumerable replicas of the statues of the great period of Athens. It is the second step in that academism from which the modern world is still suffering. The first dated from those pupils of Polycleitus, of Myron, of Phidias, and of Praxiteles who knew their trade too well.

Rome encumbers itself with statues. There are the dead and the living. All those who have held public office, high or low, want to have under their eyes the material and durable witness of

◄ Statue in relief of Neron Nero (37 to 68) in Rome.
Ruins of the Golden Palace on the Domus Aurea Hill, Rome

the fact. Far more, each one, if he can pay for it, wants to know in advance the effect that will be produced by the trough of marble in which he is to be laid away. It is not only the Imperator who is to see his military life made illustrious in the marble of the triumphal arches and columns. The centurion and the tribune surely have, in their public life, some high deed to hand down for the admiration of the future.

The sculptors of the sarcophagi devise the anecdotal bas-relief. Historical "genre," that special form of artistic degeneration, which at all times, has so comfortably kept house with academism, is invented. The great aim is to find and relate as many heroic deeds as possible in the life of the great man. On five or six metres of marble adventures are heaped up, personages, insignia, weapons, and fasces are squeezed in. Everything is episodic, and one seizes nothing of the episode; whereas in the sober Greek bas-relief where nothing was episodic, the whole signification of the scene appeared at a glance. And yet it is, above all, in these bas-reliefs that the harsh Roman genius has left its trace. There is very often a kind of sombre force and a solemnity there which affect us sharply, carrying with them a train of crushing memories — the laurels, the lictors, the consular purple. In these bas-reliefs there bursts forth a barbarous power.

Sometimes, even, in the heavy chiselled garlands where the fruits, the flowers, and the foliage accumulate and heap up like the harvests and vintages of the strong Latin Campagna, one feels the mounting of the rustic sap which Rome could not dry up and which swells in the poems of Lucretius as in an old tree that sends out green shoots again. Then the Greeks are forgotten, and the sculptors from Athens must laugh in pity before these confused poems to the riches of the earth. And doubtless they prefer the heavy imitations of themselves that are made. There are no more empty places, to be sure, no more silent passages, no longer any wave of uniting volumes that reply to one another in their constant need for musical equilibrium. But it is a disciplined orgy, even so, whose opulence is an element to be incorporated with the intoxication of the flesh rather than inscribed in the mind. The landscape background of the Roman, on the whole, affirms itself as less stylized, doubtless, but more moving and sensual than the Greek setting.

One hears the crunch of the vintagers' feet on the grapes, the oak offers armfuls of firm acorns and black leaves, the ears of wheat loaded with grains group themselves into thick sheaves, we smell the floating perfume of green boughs and the odours of the plowed soil — and the richness and density of all this sculpture are due, probably, to workmen only. In the production of the official statue maker, on the contrary, a violent confusion reigns, monotonous ennui and immobility.

Such a spirit is entirely foreign to man; it is devoted entirely to glorifying beings, things, and abstractions toward which man is not drawn by his true nature, but by prejudice, or the cult of the moment. And it was to this spirit that allegory owed the favour which it enjoyed under Roman academism. The great artist does not love allegory. If it is imposed on him, he dominates it, he drowns it in form, drawing from form itself the sense that is always in it. Allegory, on the other hand, dominates the false artist, to whom form says nothing. Allegory is the caricature of the symbol. The symbol is the living visage of the realized abstraction; allegory has to mark the presence of the abstraction by external attributes.

These cold academic studies, these manikins of bronze and of marble, these frozen gestures — always the same — these oratorical or martial attitudes which knew no change, these rolls of papyrus, these draperies, these tridents, lightning, and horns of plenty crowded themselves, heavy and tiresome, into all the public places, into forums, squares, and sanctuaries. Sarcophagi and statues were made in advance; the orator dressed in his toga, the general in his cuirass, the tribune, the quaestor,

Statue of Aesculapius, discovered in the 18th century ▶
in the temple of the Rue de Stabies. Beginning of the 2nd century B.C. Terracotta, Naples, National Archaeological Museum.

▼ *Birth of Aphrodite*,
detail of the "Ludovisi Throne", c. 470-460 B.C. Marble, h: 90 cm, I: 142 cm. Museo Nazionale Romano, Rome.

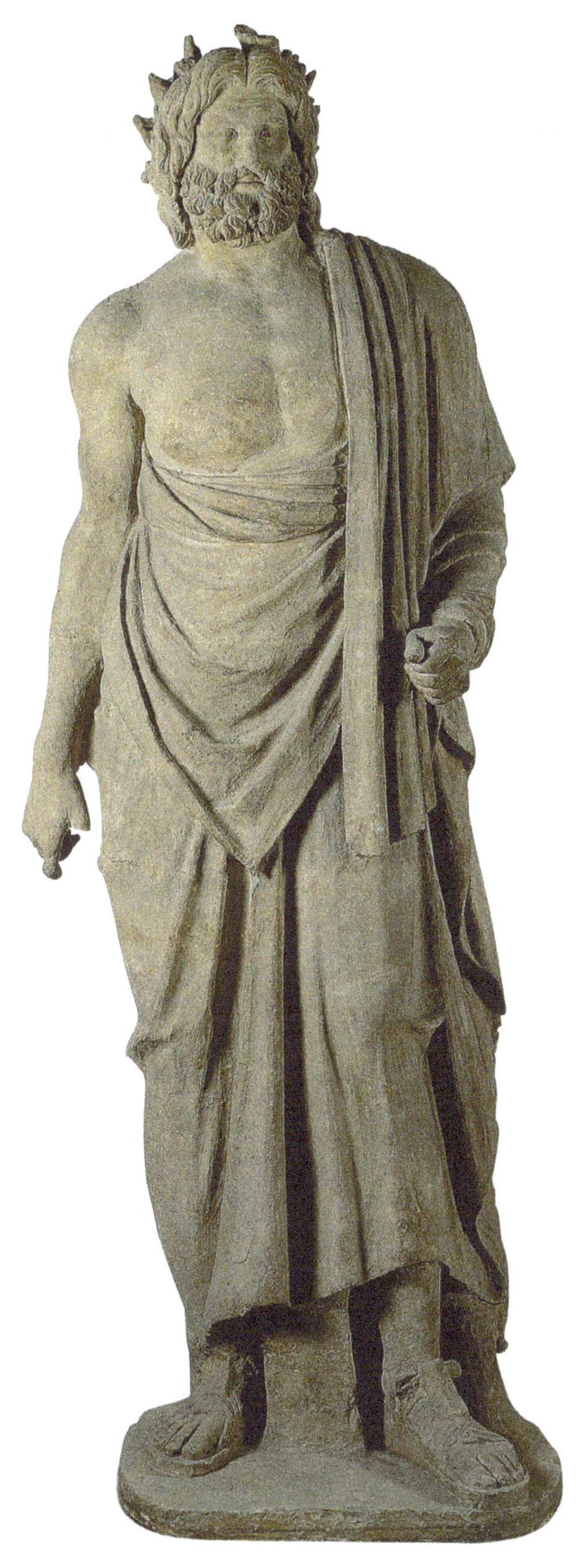

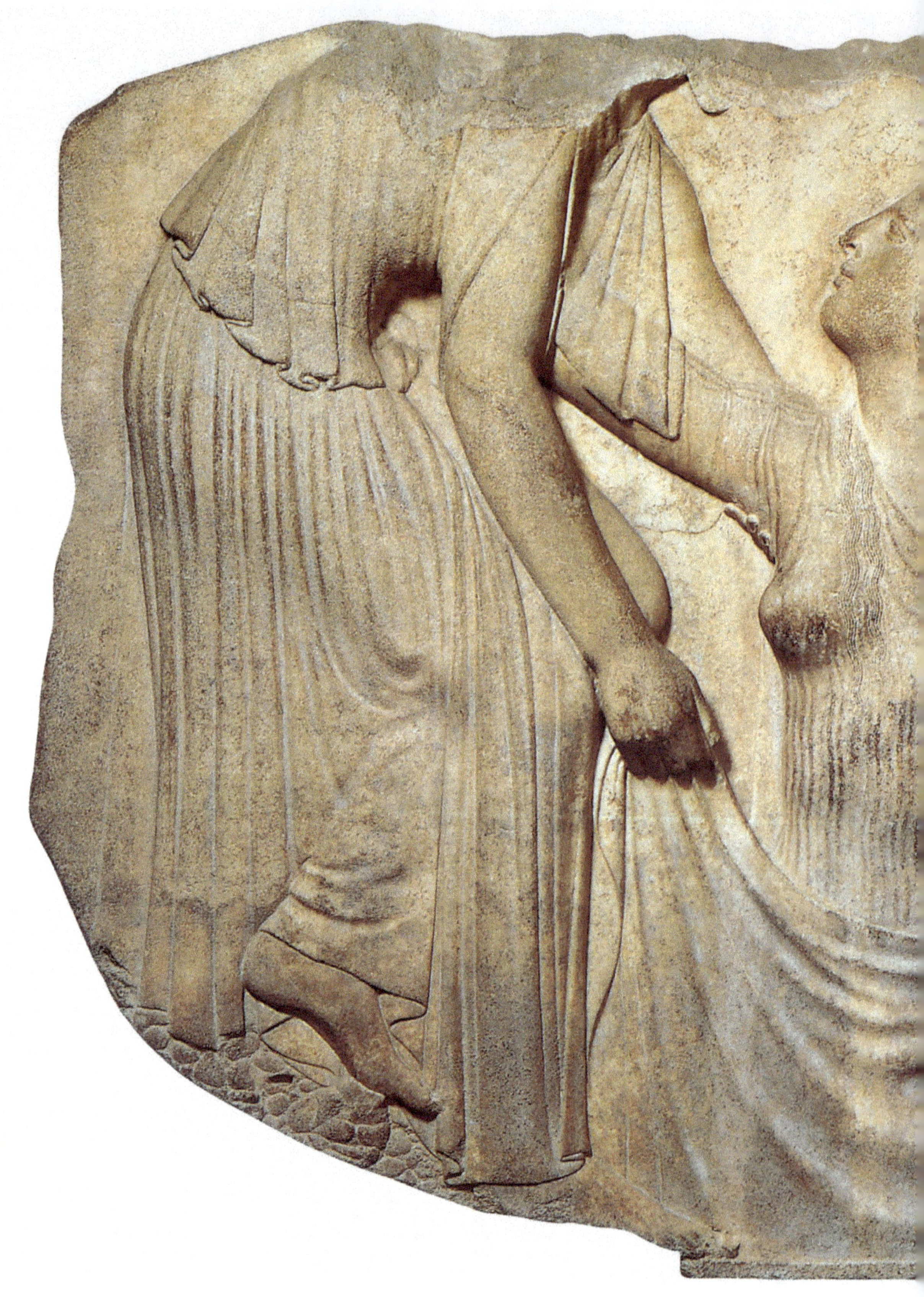

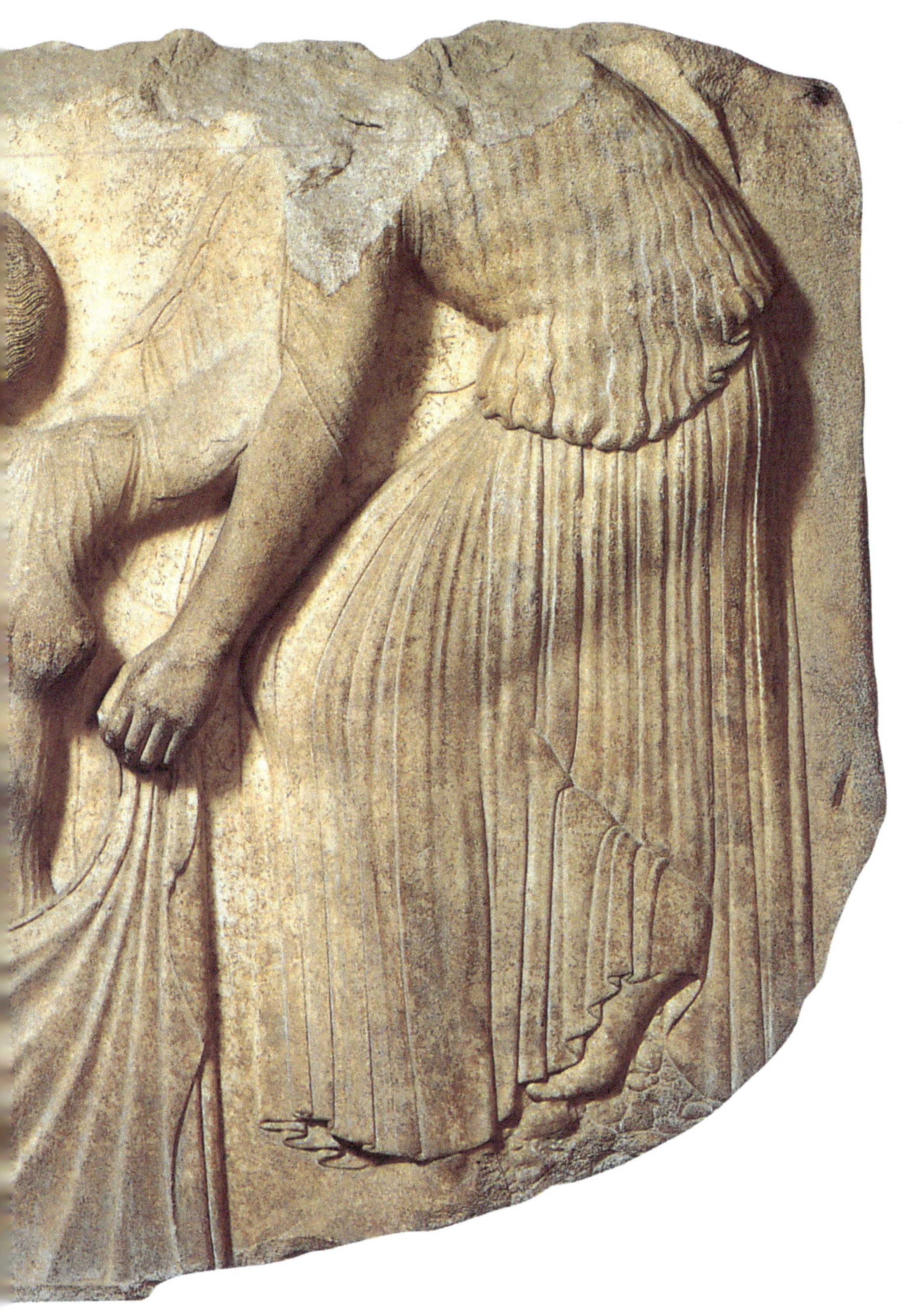

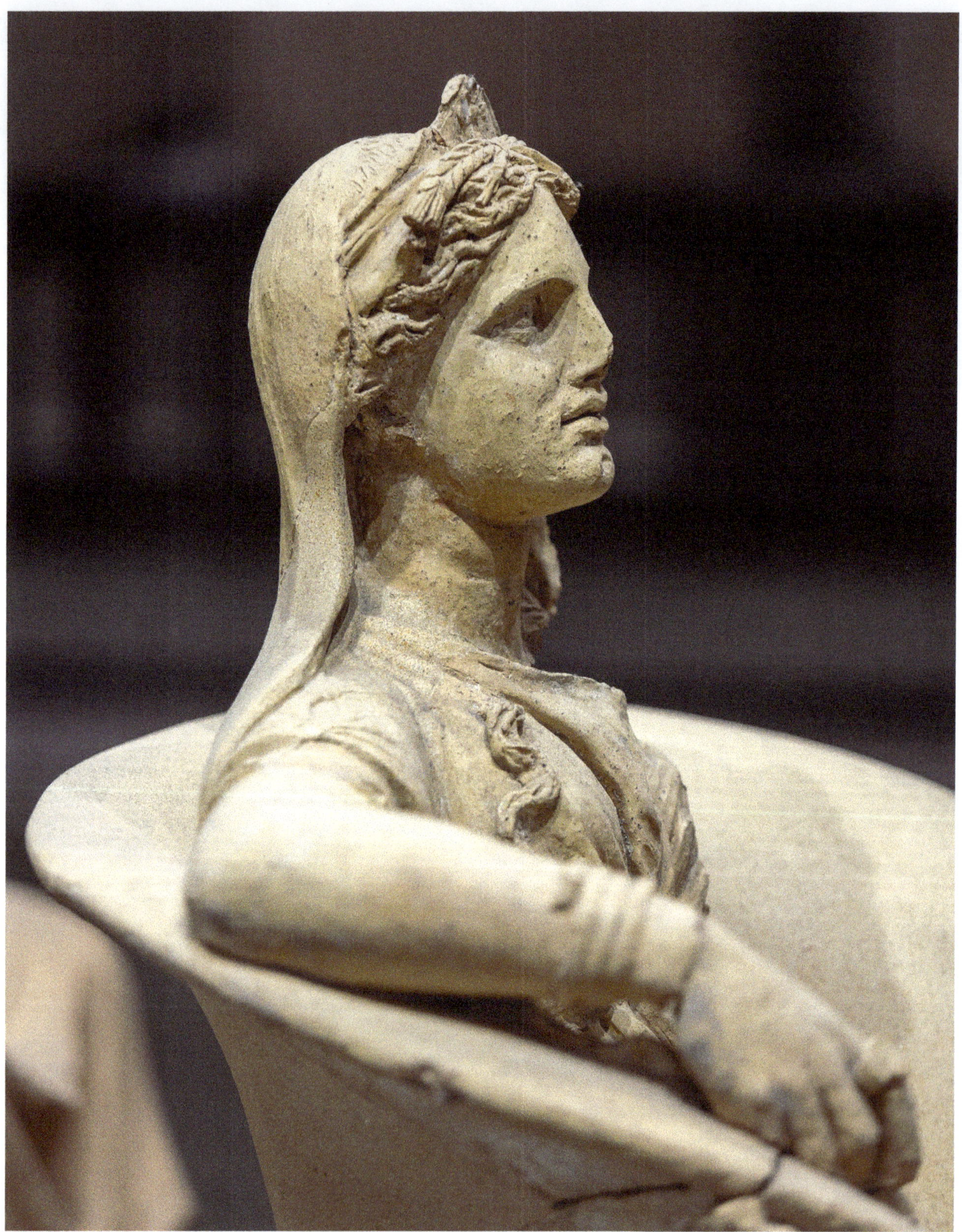

the consul, the senator, or the imperator, could be supplied at any time. The body was interchangeable. The head was screwed on to the shoulders. To recognize the personage one had to look at the face, which would sometimes be placed too high to be distinguishable. It was the only thing that did not have the appearance of having come from the factory. It alone responded to a need for truth, an obscure and material need, but a sincere one. It was made only after the order had been given and from the person who ordered it; thereafter, the artist and the model collaborated honestly.

There is something implacable about all these Roman portraits. There is no convention, but also no fantasy. Man or woman, emperor or noble, the model is followed feature by feature, from the bone structure of the face to the grain of the skin, from the form of the hair dressing to the irregularities of the noses and the brutality of the mouths. The marble cutter is attentive, diligent, and of complete probity. He does not think even of emphasizing the descriptive elements of the model's face, he wants to make it a likeness. There is not the least attempt at generalizing, no attempt at lies or flattery or satire — no concern with psychology and little character, in the descriptive sense of the word. There is less of penetration than of care for exactitude. If the artist does not lie, neither does

the model. These are historical documents, from the real Caesars of Rome to the adventurers of Spain or of Asia, from deified monsters to Stoic emperors. Where is the classic type of the "profile like a medal" in these heads? They may be heavy or delicate, square, sharp-featured, or round, at times dreamy, often wicked, but they are always beaten old centurions, or crowned hetairies who are not even pretty. Some of these heads, certainly, through their quality of attention, and the intensity with which life concentrates in them, by their density and mass, by the pitiless pursuit of the profound modelling which the bone structure of the interrogated face possesses by chance and reveals to the sculptor, are of a powerful beauty. In the statue of the Great Vestal, for example, immediate truth attains the stage of typical truth: then the whole of Rome, with its domination of itself, and the weight it laid on the world, appears in this strong and grave woman; it is as solid as the citadel, as safe as the hearth, without humanity, without tenderness, and without weakness, until the day when slowly, deeply, irresistibly, it is to have plowed its furrow.

We must turn our back on the temples; give scarcely a glance to the massive arches and columns of triumph. Around them the brutal mounting of the processions lifts the power of Rome to an empyrean no higher than their summit. The Rome, which wanted to be and believed itself to be an artist, put the whole of its native genius into the marble portraits and into certain bas-reliefs of startling authority and ruggedness.

◀ *Statue of a woman* at the Baths of Diocletian Diocletian, (v. 244-to 311), Thermae Diocletiani, Rome.

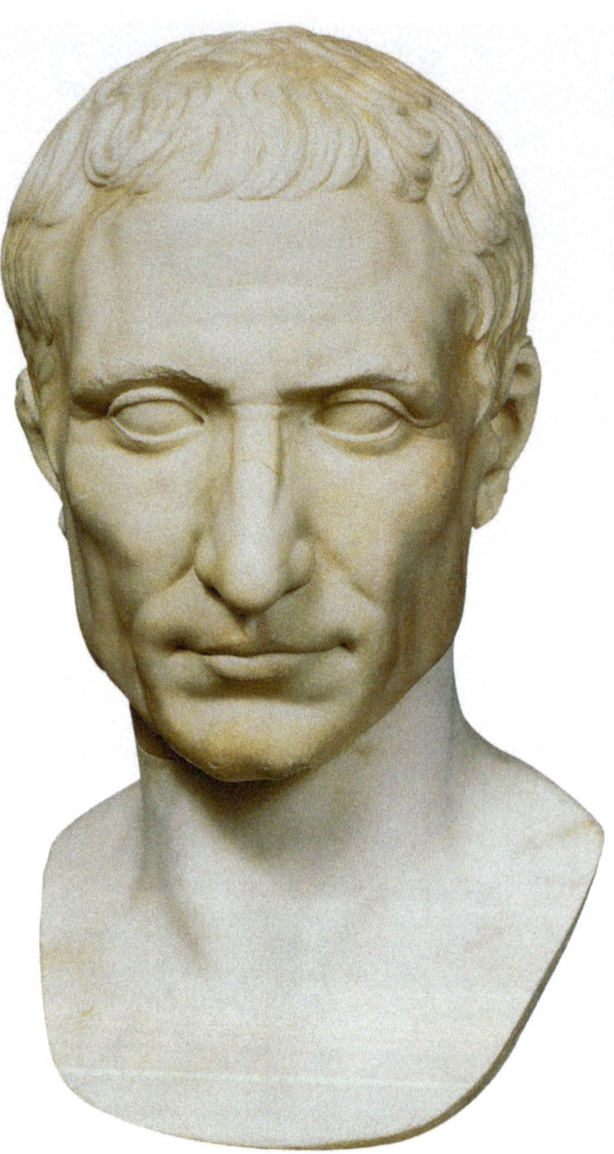

Marble Portrait of Julius Cesar, ▶
born in Rome on 12 July 100 BC-Died on 15 March 44
BC, General, politician. Vatican Museum.

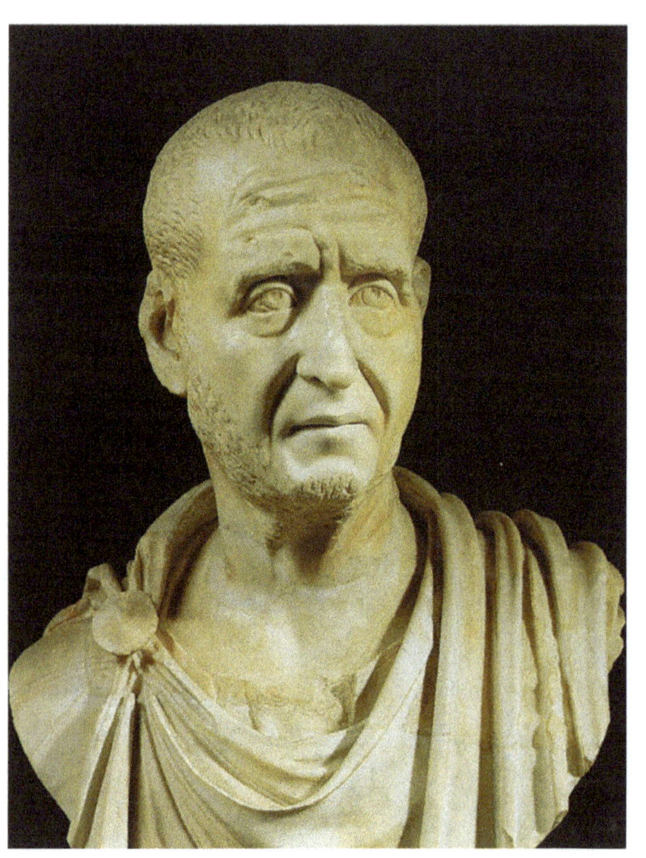

◀ *Portrait of Trajan Decius*, 249-251 AD, marble,
H: 78 cm. Rome, Museo Capitolino.

Portrait of Augustus, ▶
born Caius Octavius on 23 September 63 BC in Rome,
he bore the name of Imperator Caesar Augustus when
he died on 19 August 14 A.D. in Nola. First Roman
Emperor, from 16 January 27 B.C. to 19 August 14 A.D.

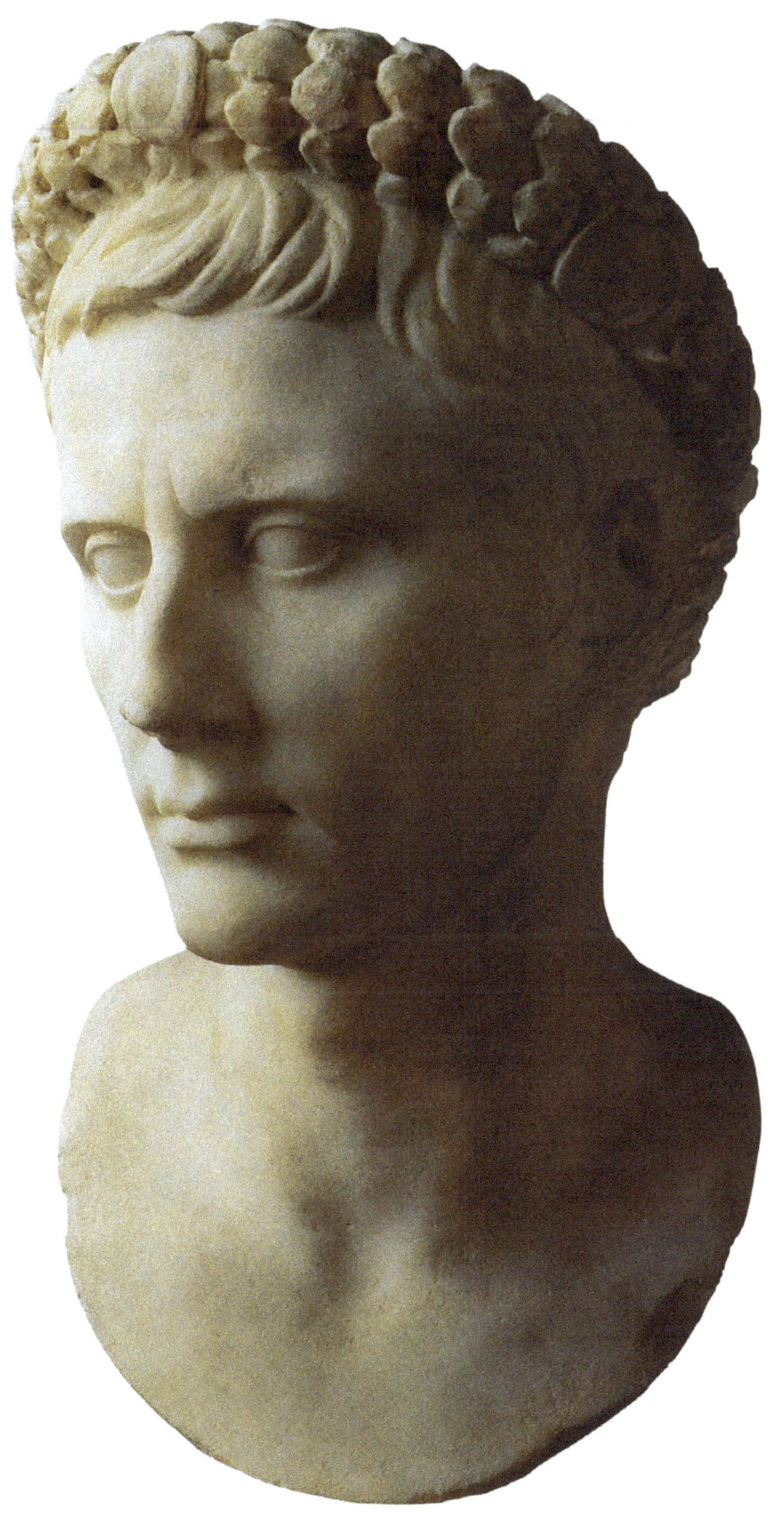

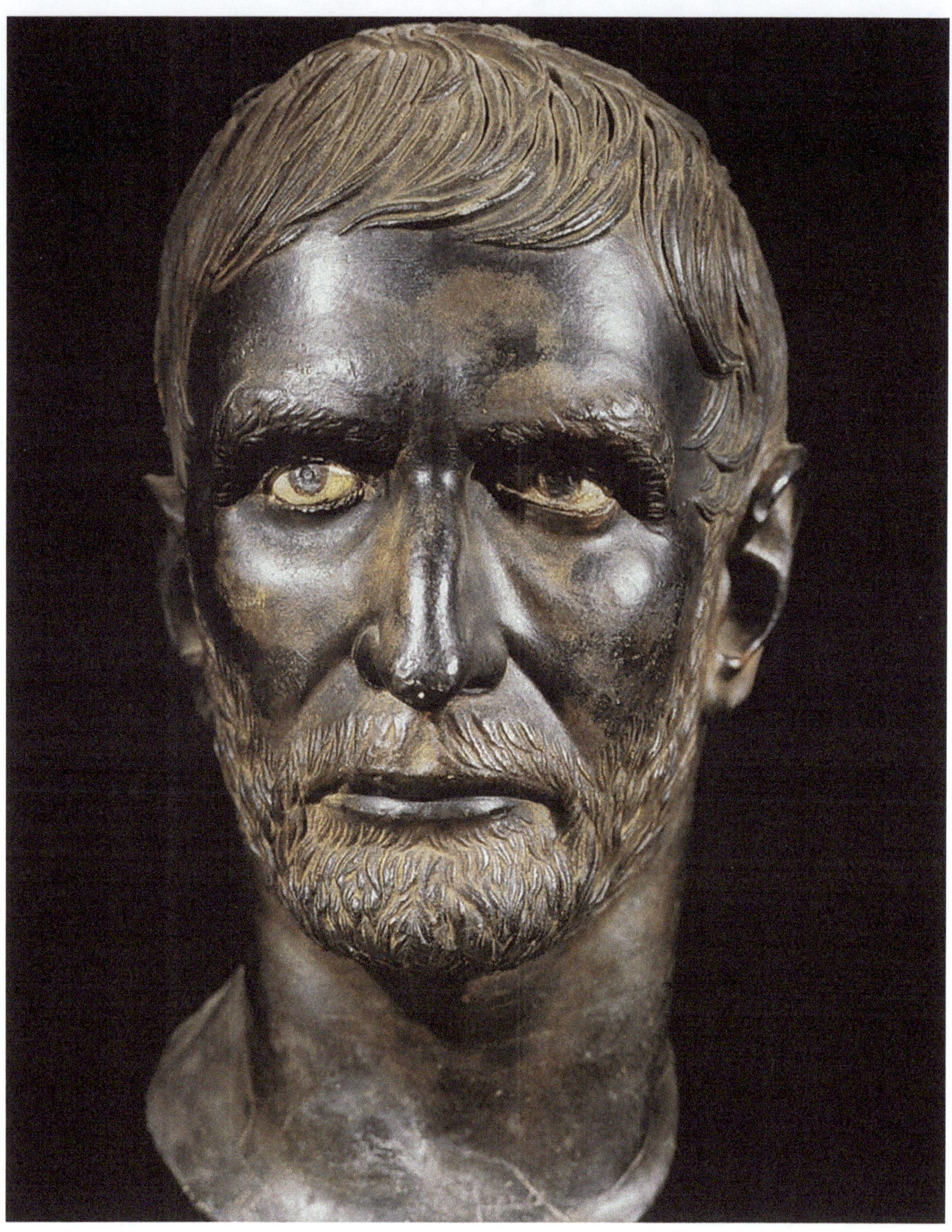

▼ *Bronze Statue* (process of lost wax) representing a pugiliste
at rest, known as the pugiliste of the thermal baths. Rome,
Roman National Museum, Octagonal hall, Old Planetarium.

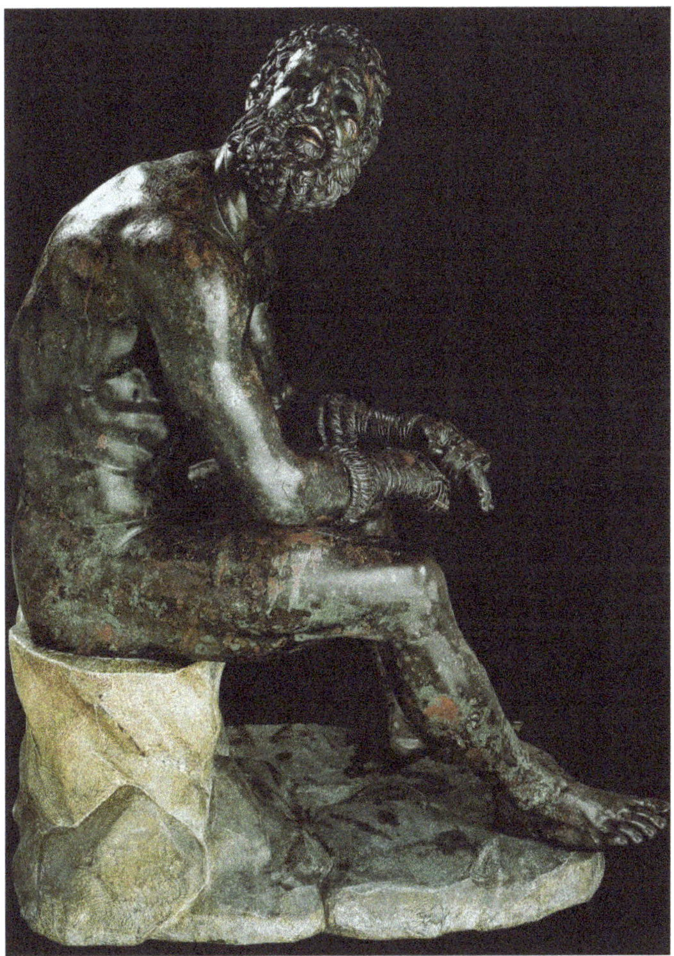

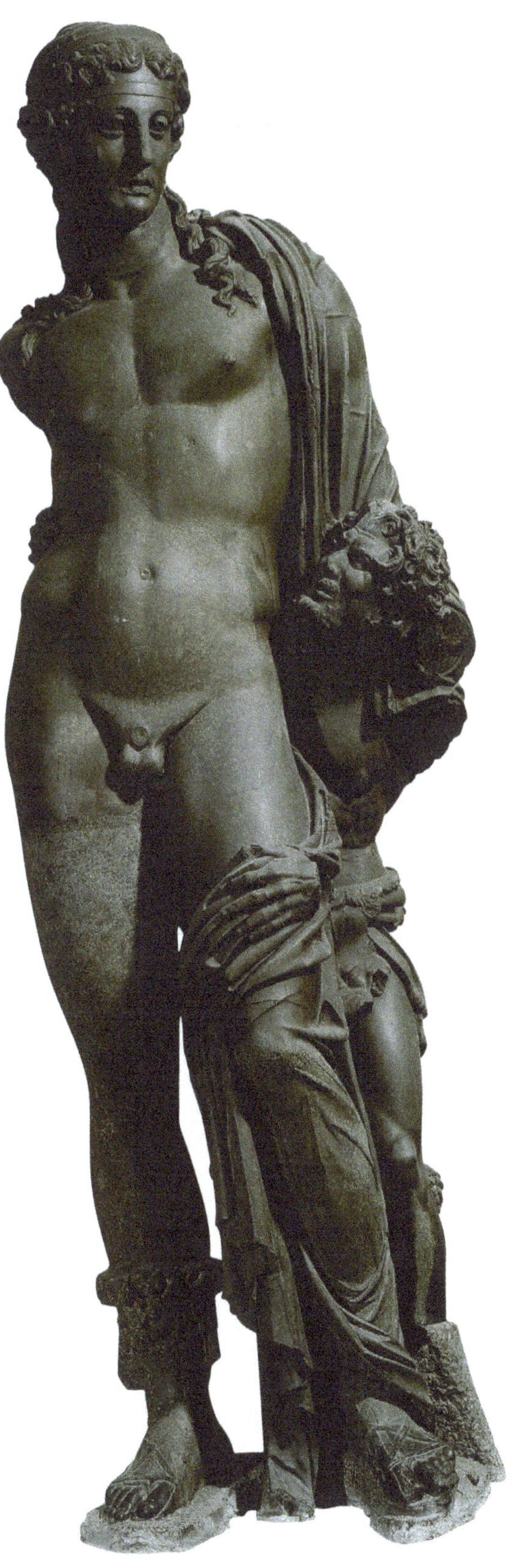

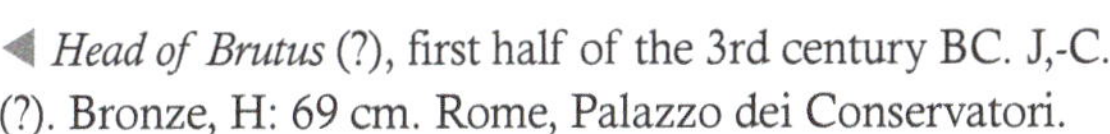

◀ *Head of Brutus* (?), first half of the 3rd century BC. J,-C.
(?). Bronze, H: 69 cm. Rome, Palazzo dei Conservatori.

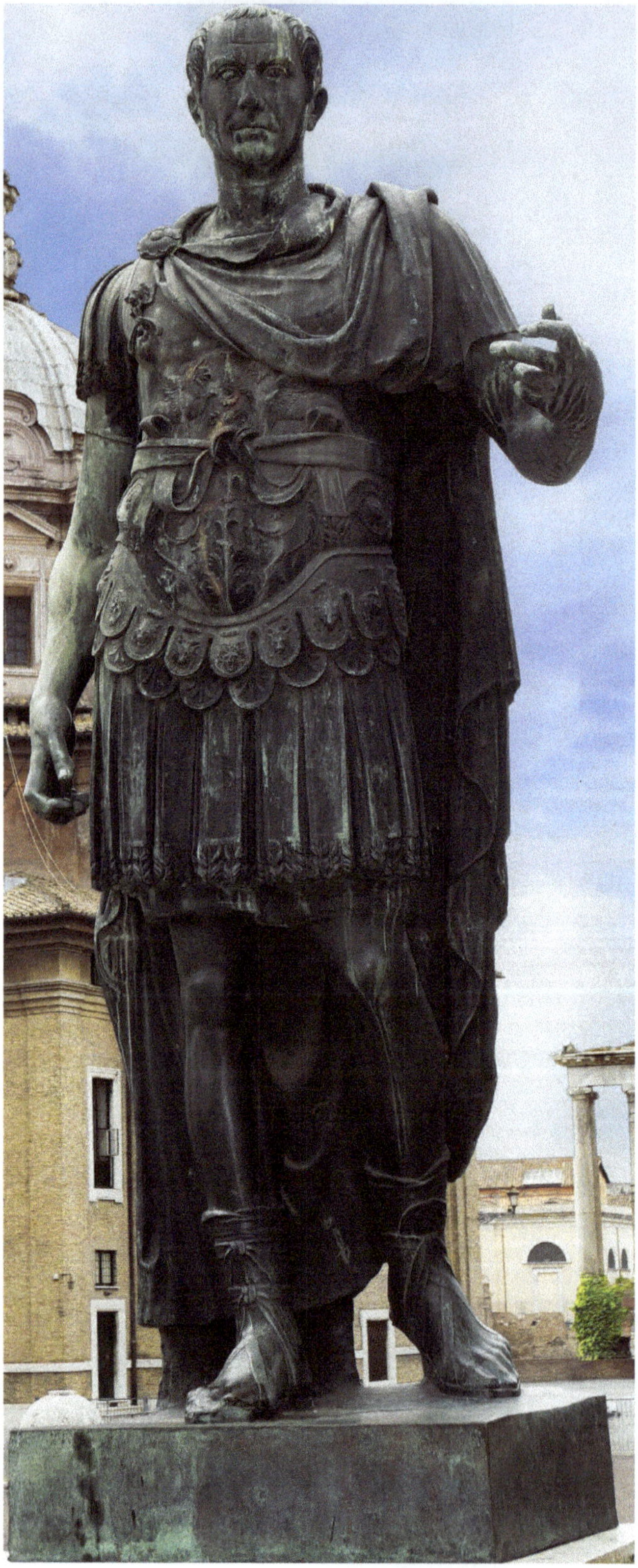

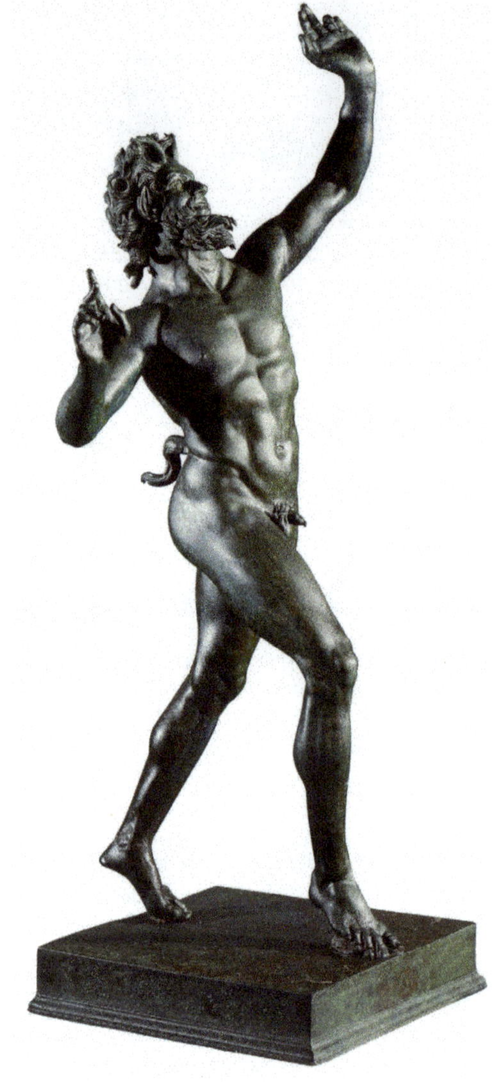

◄ *Statue of Julius Cesar* in front of the temple of
Venus Genetrix Rome.

▲ *Dancing fauna*. Bronze. H: 71 cm.
Naples, National Archaeological Museum.

Statue of Marcus Holconius Rufus. ▶
Marble. Naples, National Archaeological Museum.
This prestigious citizen of Pompeii was a
military tribune, priest of Augustus and several
times duumvir.

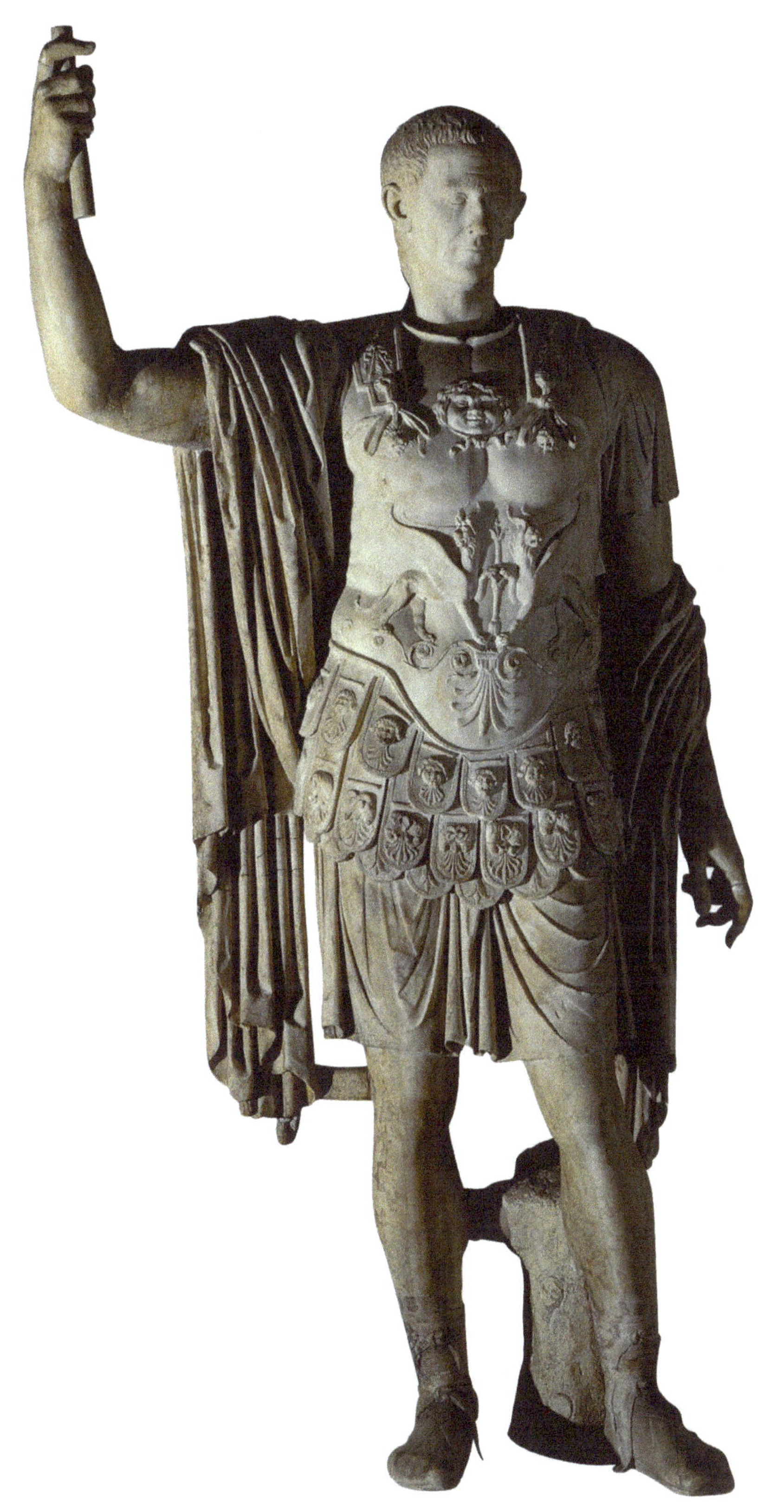

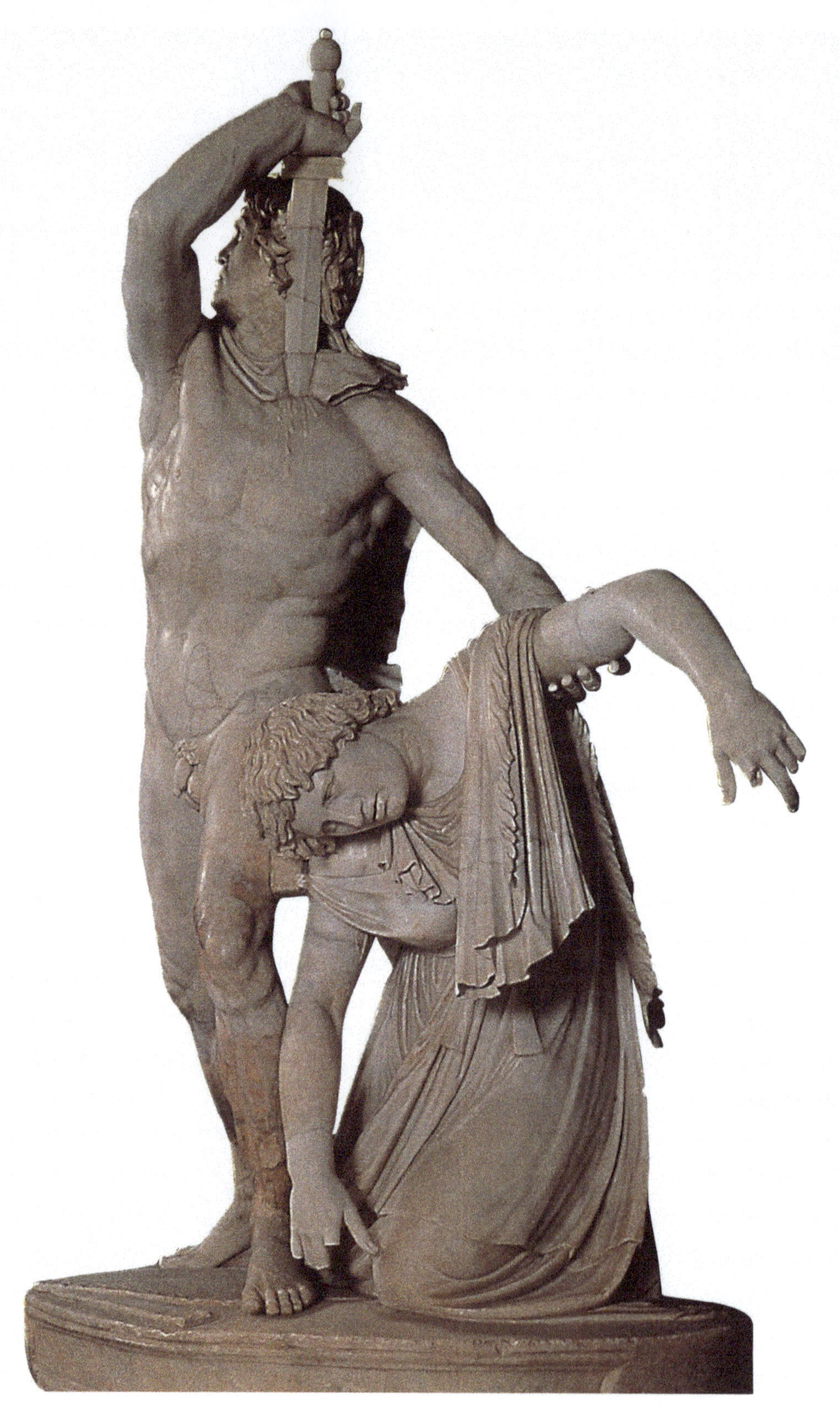

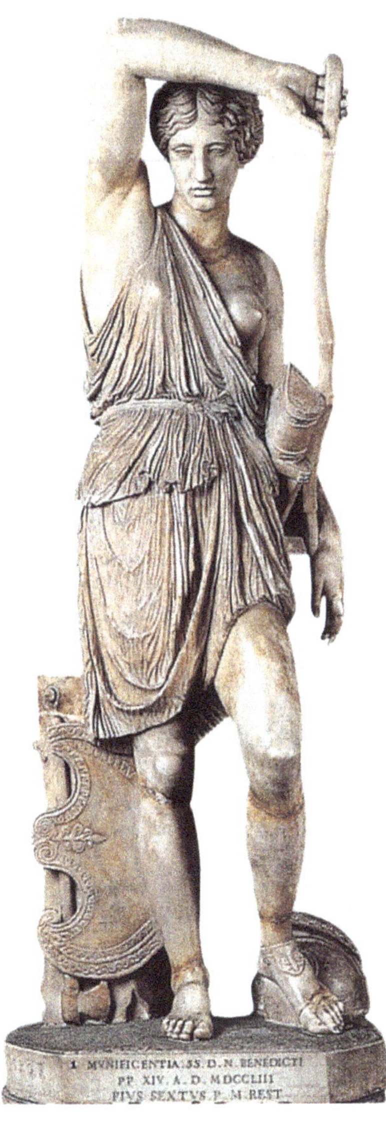

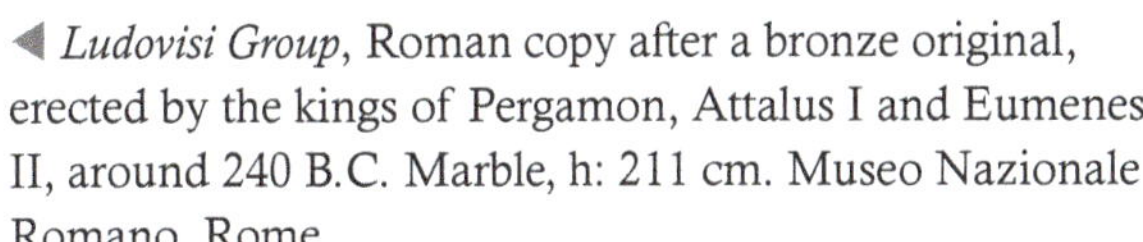

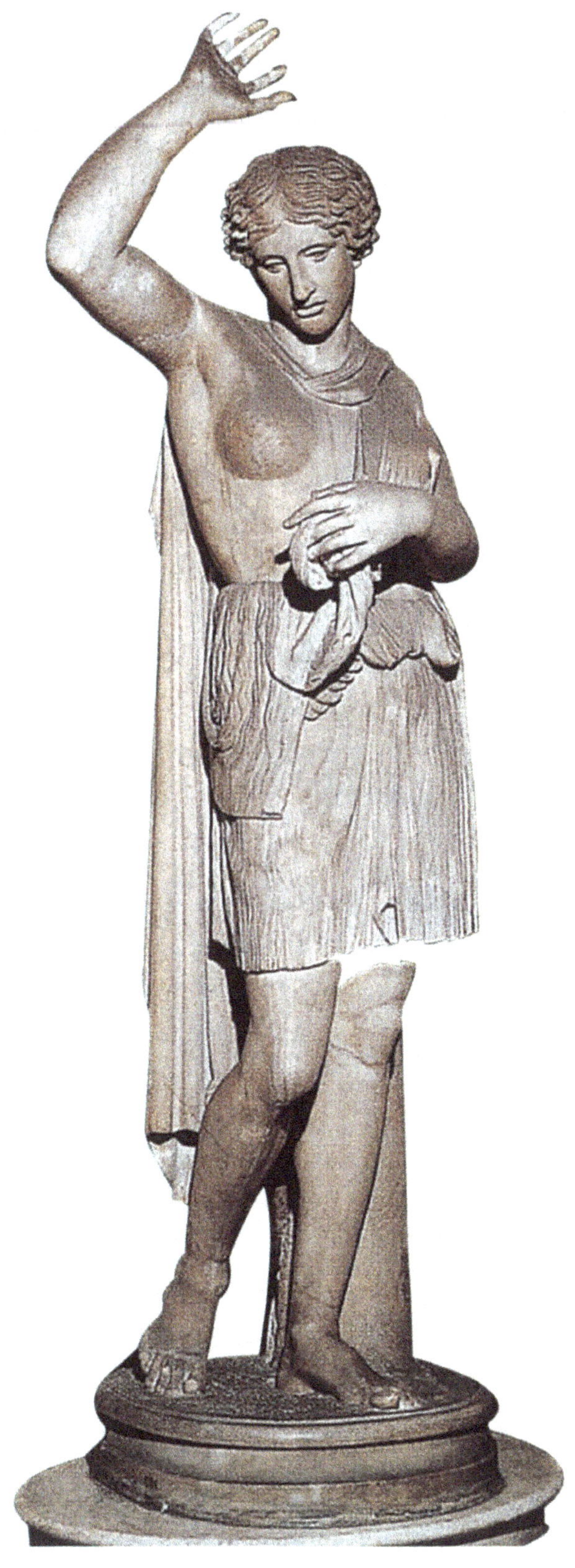

◀ *Ludovisi Group*, Roman copy after a bronze original, erected by the kings of Pergamon, Attalus I and Eumenes II, around 240 B.C. Marble, h: 211 cm. Museo Nazionale Romano, Rome

▲ *Mattei Amazon bending the Arch*, copy after a Greek original by Polykleitos created c. 440-430 B.C. Marble. Musei Capitolini, Rome.

▶ *Wounded Amazon*, Roman copy after a Greek original by Polykleitos created c. 440-430 B.C. Marble, h: 202 cm. Musei Capitolini, Rome.

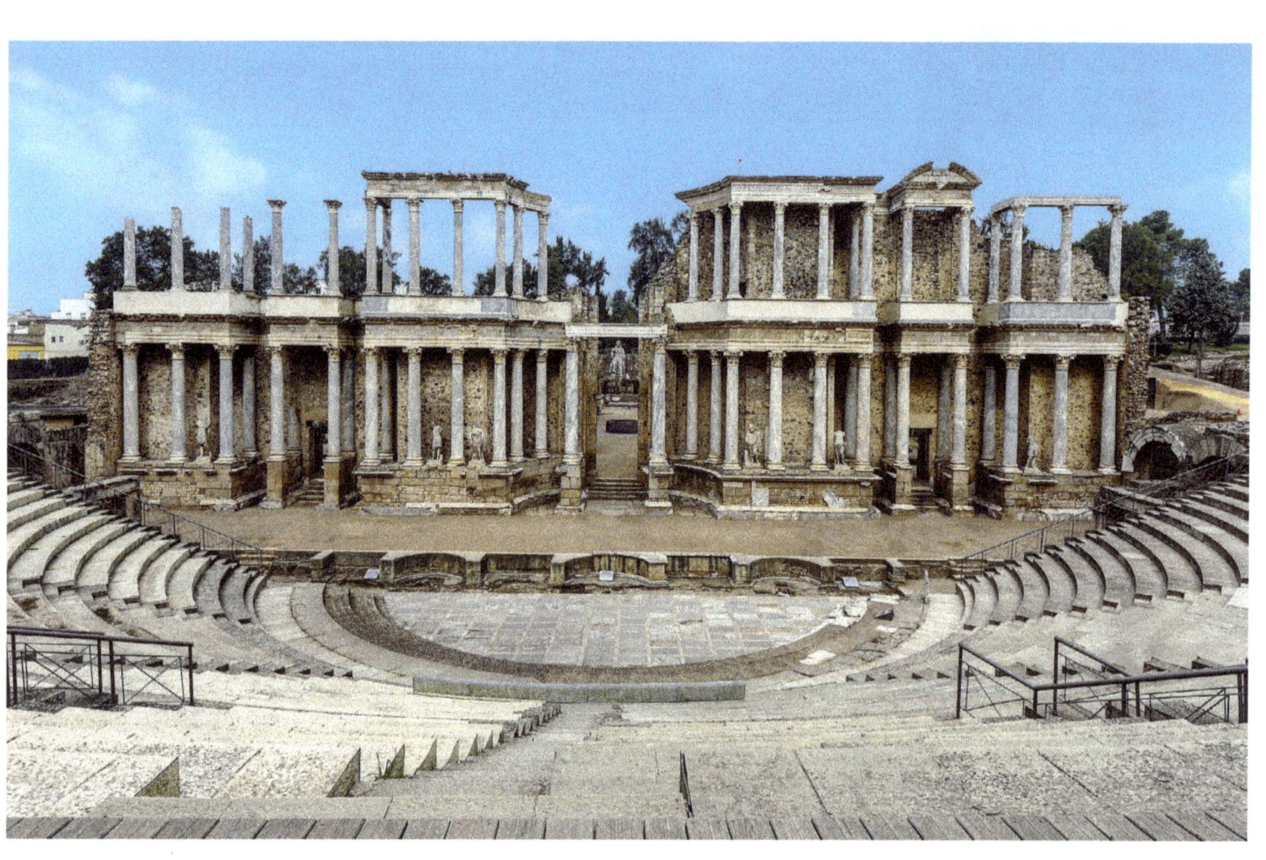

ARCHITECTURE

In architecture, too, Roman builders learnt much from their Etruscan neighbours, from whom they borrowed the characteristic form of their temples, and perhaps also the prominent use of the arch and the vault. But the stream of the Etruscan influence was met by a counter-current from the south, where the Greek colonies in Campania provided a natural channel by which Hellenic ideas reached the Latins; and Roman architects soon abandoned the purely Etruscan type of temple for one which closely followed western Greek models. The conquest of the later Republic, however, brought them into more direct contact with the art of Greece proper.

Beginning from 212 B.C., when Marcellus despoiled Syracuse of its principal statues, every victorious general adorned his triumph with masterpieces of Greek art, whether of sculpture or of painting, and, when Philhellenism became the ruling fashion at Rome, wealthy connoisseurs formed private collections drawn from the Greek provinces – Greek craftsmen, moreover, were employed in the decoration of palaces of the Roman nobles and capitalists. Except in portraiture, there was nothing characteristically Roman in the art which flourished in Rome in the time of Caesar and Cicero.

In the art, as in literature of the Augustan age, classicism was the dominant note, and the naturalism so congenial to Italian temperament was repressed, though never extinguished. The result of this was that under the Julio-Claudian dynasty academic tradition filled the place of inspiration, and Roman art failed to discover its vocation. A change came under the Flavian emperors. The painters who decorated with fairy landscapes the walls of Roman palaces, untrammelled by the conventions of official art, introduced into Rome a summary method of working, which has much in common with that of a modern school and the sculptors of the Flavian period laid to heart the lesson taught by their successful "illusionism". We are entitled to rank this Flavian art as the specific creation of imperial Rome.

◀ *Amphitheatre of Merida* The amphitheatre measures 126 meters of large axle, 65 meters of small axle and can accommodate 15 000 people. Reign of Auguste 8 BC. Merida Spain.

▼ *Colosseum* began between 70 and 72 A.D. Completed in 80 under Titus. Accommodating between 50 000 and 75 000 spectators. Rome, Italy.

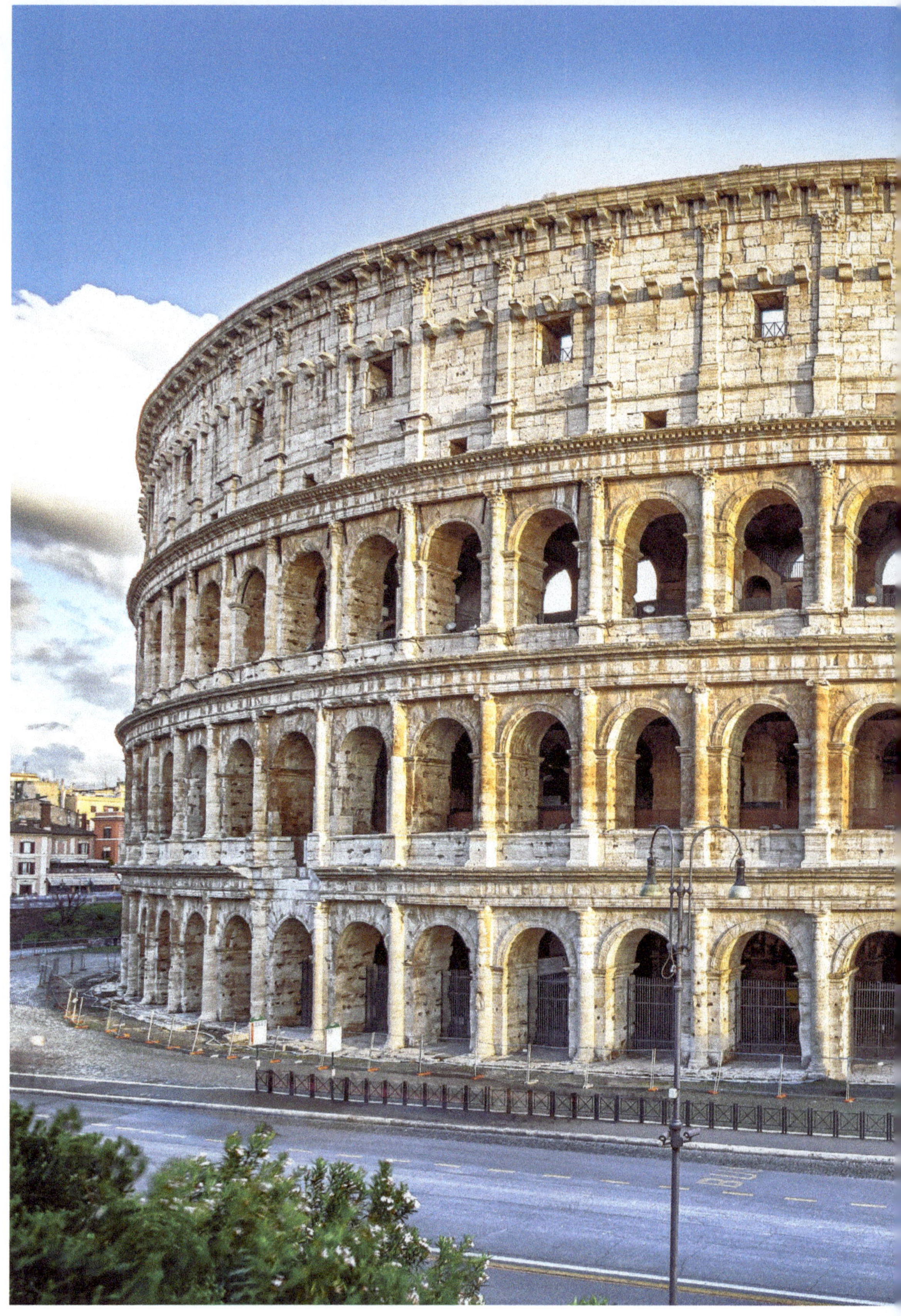

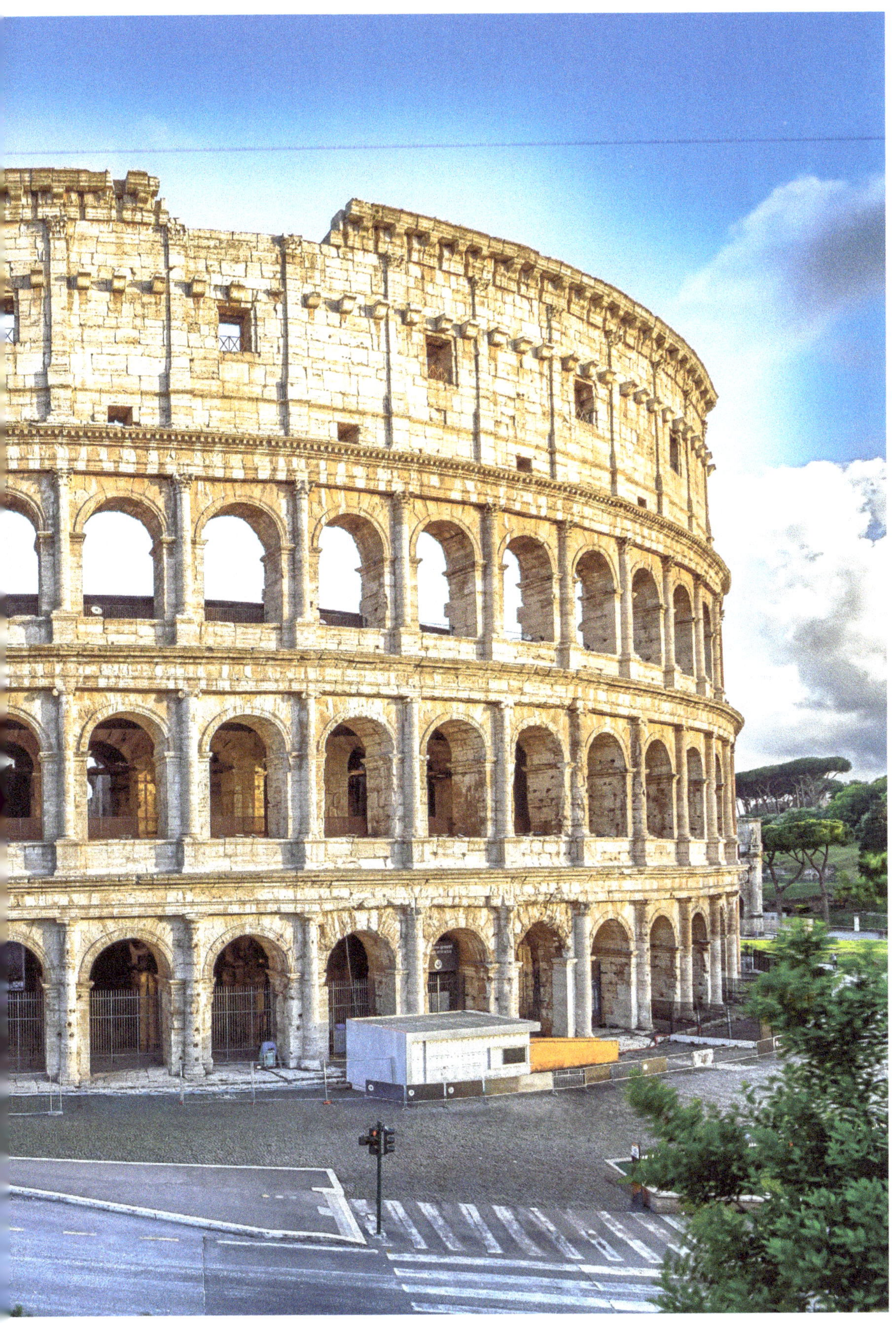

But this phase was of short duration and the Roman spirit triumphed under Trajan and found its characteristic expression in the "epic of stone" with which his column is adorned. Historical art achieved no less a triumph in the great frieze from Trajan's Forum, and in the panels of the arch of Benevento. Imposing as these works are, they suffer from the defects incidental to an art which endeavours to express too much. Overcharged with detail, and packed with meanings which reveal themselves only to patient study, they lack the spacious and reposeful character of Greek art.

It was natural that the imperial influences which, as we have seen, acted strongly upon Roman literature and sculpture, should exert themselves even more strongly upon their architecture. Instances of this will, of course, occur to everyone who has visited Rome, or who has seen the wonderful display of Roman power at Verona, Nîmes, Saint-Rémy-de-Provence and Arles in France at El Djem in Tunesia, at Pola in Croatia, or at Baalbec in Lebanon.

These stupendous monuments of power will at once impress their history vividly upon the mind; but perhaps it may be suggestive if we turn aside for a moment to remark upon the vast aqueducts which span the Campagna round Rome. It is often asked why the Romans spent so much wealth and labour in erecting these vast ranges of arches, when they knew perfectly well how to conduct water in pipes, and did so within the walls of their metropolis to a considerable extent. An answer to this question will be found directly

when we see it at the point of view from which we are now considering Roman art. When viewed in this light we shall be inclined to take what may be called "a political view" of the construction of the aqueducts, as intended mainly to display imperial power, and to give employment to vast numbers of architects and workmen.

The specific achievement of the Roman architect was the artistic application of a new set of principles – those which are expressed in the arch, the vault and the dome. The rectilinear buildings of the Greeks with their direct vertical supports gave place to the vaulted structures in which lateral thrust was called into play. The aesthetic effect of the curves thus brought into prominence was well understood by the Romans; and they were the inventors of the decorative combination of the Greek orders with the arcade. More than this, the erection of vaults and domes of wide span, rendered possible by the use of concrete, gave to the Roman architect the opportunity of dealing artistically with internal spaces. A simple yet grandiose example of this may be found in the Pantheon of Hadrian.

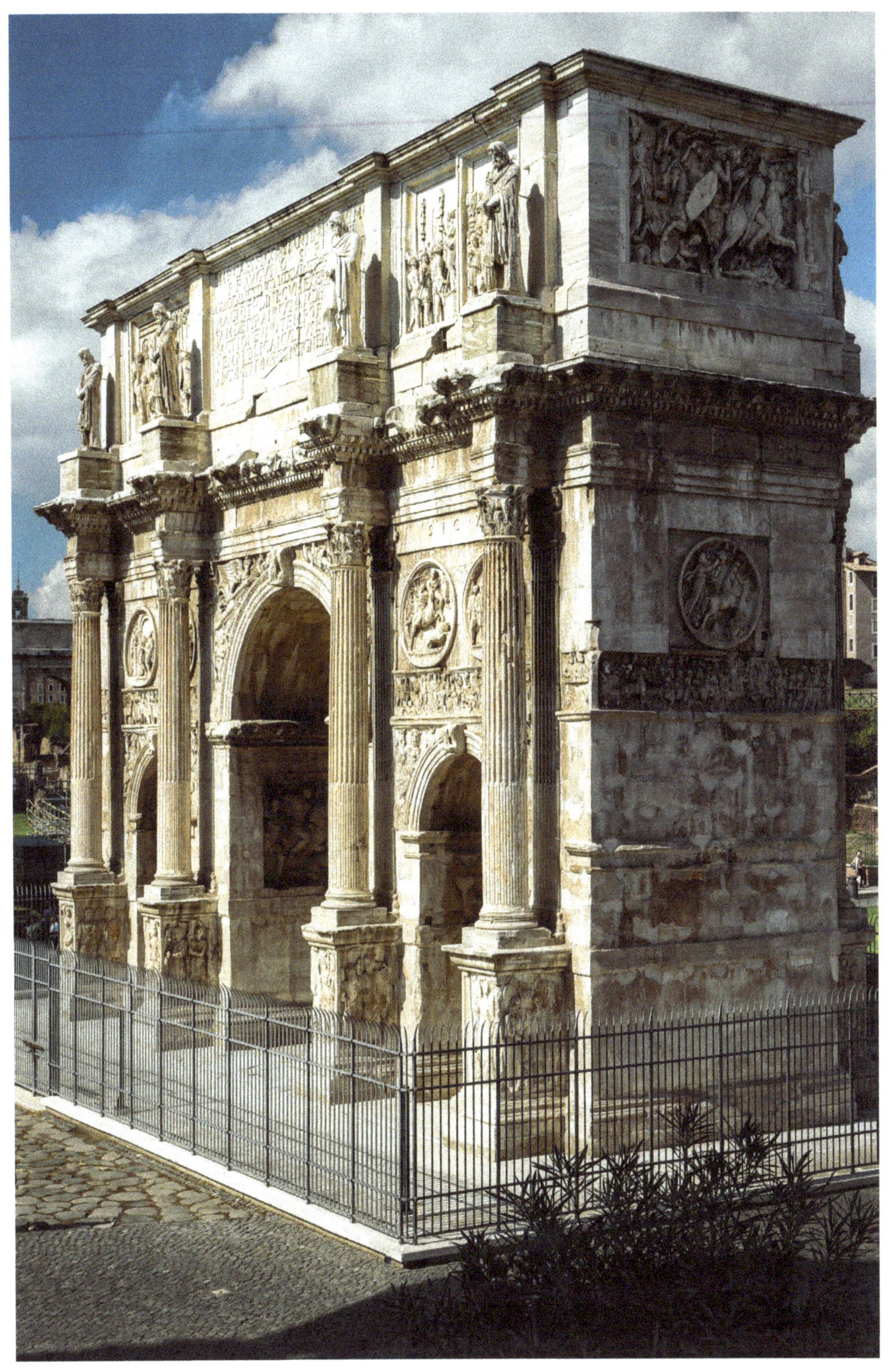

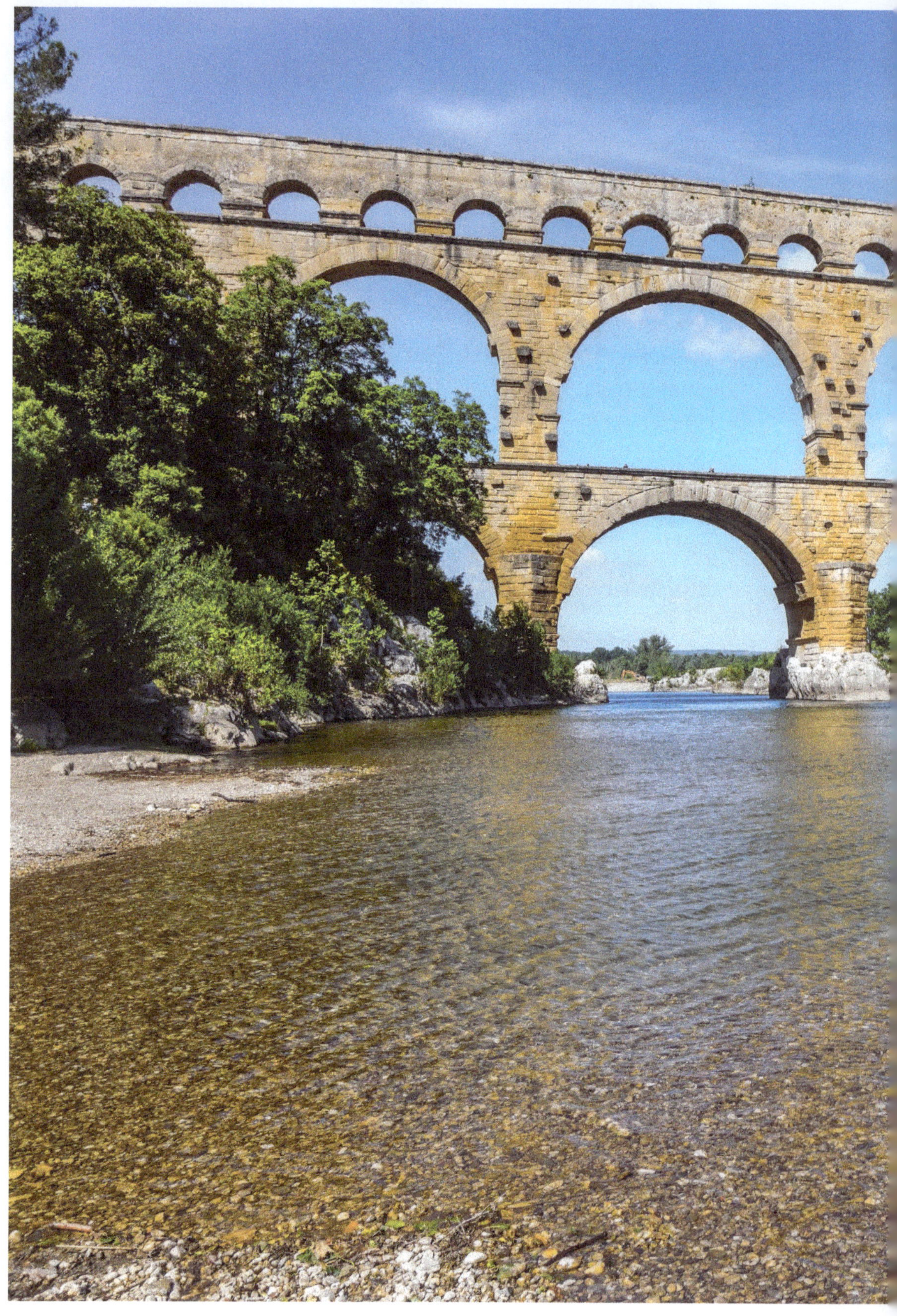

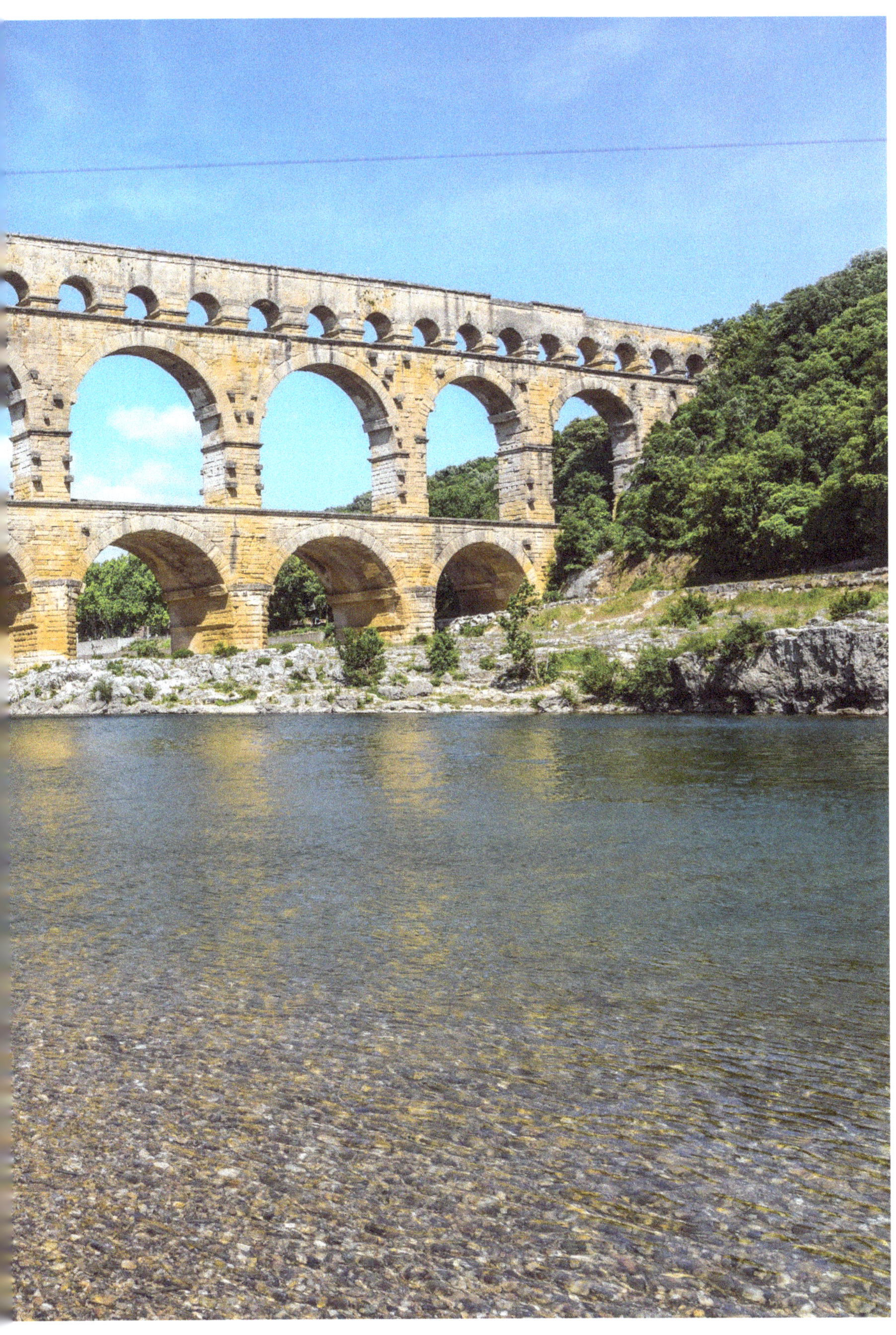

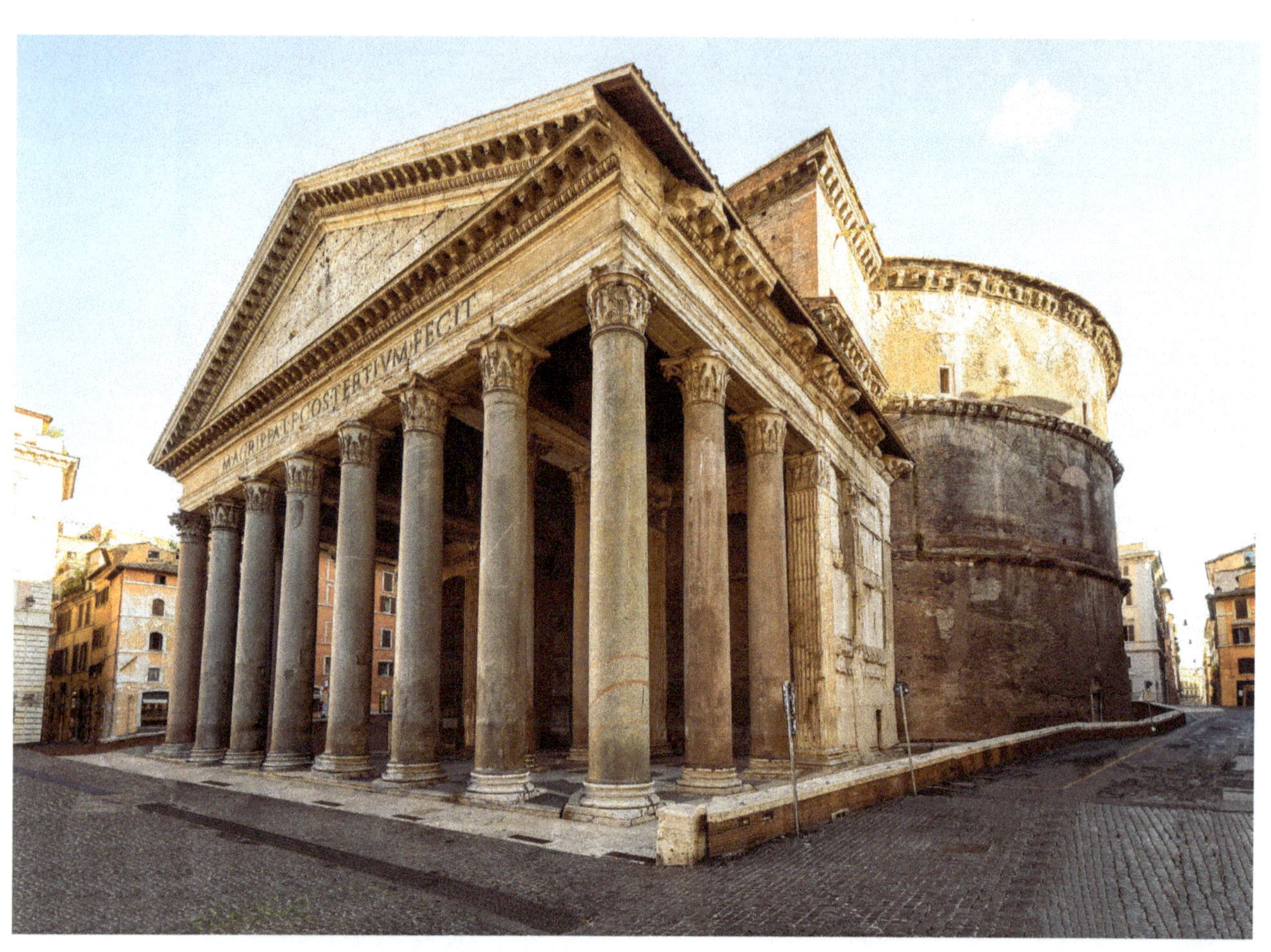

Circular buildings were a common feature in Italian architecture and the theme was repeated with many variations, from the well-known circular temple in the Forum Boarium to the fantastic structure with broken outlines at Baalbeck.

The official religious architecture is flooded with ornaments, quadrigas, bas-reliefs, allegories, and false columns. The Corinthian column which, with the leaves of its capital crushed by the entablature, was so illogical that the Greeks hardly ever used it seems invented to permit the Romans to display, in stupefying contrast, the lack of artistic intelligence of those among them who were entrusted with preserving the city of art. As soon as they use ornaments, their architecture loses its beauty, because it loses its logic.

There are no ornaments on his aqueducts, his bridges, or his thermae, very few on his amphitheatres, and these are, with those positive portraits, his only real works of art. Bare, straight, categorical, accepting their role, they present to us their terrible walls, piles of matter gilded by the southern fire, crackled and whitened by the frosts of the north. They present their aerial vaults on cyclopean pillars, the lines of giant arches bestriding the valleys and the swamps, bursting through rocky barriers or sealing them — as sure, in their vertical rise or their progression, as cliffs

Pantheon of Rome built by order of Agrippa during the 1st century B.C., rebuilt under Hadrian (early 2nd century A.D.). Largest dome of all antiquity 43.30 m in diameter inside. Rome, Italy.

or as herds of primitive monsters. The goal toward which they aim gives them a look of implacability. They have the inflexibility of mathematics, the force of the will, the authority of pride.

They have the lightness of the foliage that quivers at the top of the trees, sixty feet above the ground. The arch, the vaults of various kinds, the corridors, and the cupolas, a thousand blocks of granite are, for twenty centuries, suspended in the air like leaves. They cannot crumble before the infiltration of water and the assault of the winds and the sun have uprooted their trunks; they have an air of being natural growths which would outlast all winters. To petrify the depth of the azure, the depth of the tree top! It needed the imagination of man to realize the miracle of offering to the crowds, as their perpetual shelter, the curves which bent over the curve of the earth. It needed the audacity of man to suspend matter in space by its own weight, to stick stones to one another by leaving so little space between them that they cannot fall, to check their tendency to separate by thickening the pillars that bear them, until a point of absolute solidity is reached.

The Roman wall is one of the great things of history. And, as it is Might, it is Right. It seems to be uninterrupted, it holds forever, even when split and fissured. The fall of a thousand stones does not shake it. For ten centuries all the houses of Rome were built of the stones of the Colosseum. The Colosseum has not changed its form. The Roman wall remains identical with itself everywhere. The pavement of the roads, which for two hundred leagues pursues its rigid march, is only a wall lying on the earth to embrace it and enslave it. The arch of the bridges, which is only a wall bent like the wood of a bow, draws taut the passive bowstring of the rivers. The wall of the aqueducts, hollowed out like the beds of the rivers themselves, carried their waters in a straight line wherever the aedile wants them to go. High and bare, the outer wall of the theatre prevents those whose appetite or rebellion is to be overcome from peering into the free expanse of the horizon. The wall of the circuses, continuous and compact as a circle of bronze, incloses the bloody orgy within the geometrical rigour of a law.

It was in Rome that the applications of the Asiatic vault were the most various, its use the most frequent, its employment the most methodical. The vault, in Chaldea and in Assyria, had lengthened itself out, weighed down on the palaces and houses or swelled above them, and hung over the cities. In Rome it is the very base of every utilitarian construction, and the greater part of the architectonic forms derive from its presence — the arches of the bridges, the portals, the corridors around the circuses, the immensity of the halls made possible by the might the height of the edifice, the circular monuments — images of the horizon, of the plains bearing the cupola of the sky.

The Tombs of Cecilia Metella, the Mole of Hadrian, and the Pantheon of Agrippa especially, are epitomes of the force of Rome and of the severe and savage ring of hills, the circus in the centre of which it is built. At the top of the Pantheon a circular opening lets in the light of heaven. It falls as if regretfully, and never succeeds in illuminating the furthest corners. Rome is self-willed and closed. It is only into the stone circuses that the sun entered in a flood, to light up the spectacles which the tamed world gave to Rome while it waited till it should gather up in the city its hatred, revolt, and thirst for purification. Panem et Circenses! The Colosseum is nothing but the formula in stone of the monstrous needs of the king-people. The patrician no longer has war at his command to occupy the plebeian. Here is bread — here are circuses, in which a whole city can be seated and which are built in such a way that from each of the seats one can witness the death struggle of that city. Never has there been seen under the heavens a theatre better arranged for presenting the spectacle of a suicide than that one.

The equilibrium of Rome had not the spontaneous and philosophic character of the equilibrium of Athens, and this does not result so much from the multiform extent of the Roman Empire as from the depth of its moral anarchy. Greece, while at war with Persia, was much nearer to harmony than Rome was at the very hour when she decreed peace. Her repose, her art, her pleasure, even, were of an administrative order. The struggle of interests, the rivalry of classes, and the social disorder continued from

Amphitheatre of Jerash ▶
2nd century A.D. Jordan.

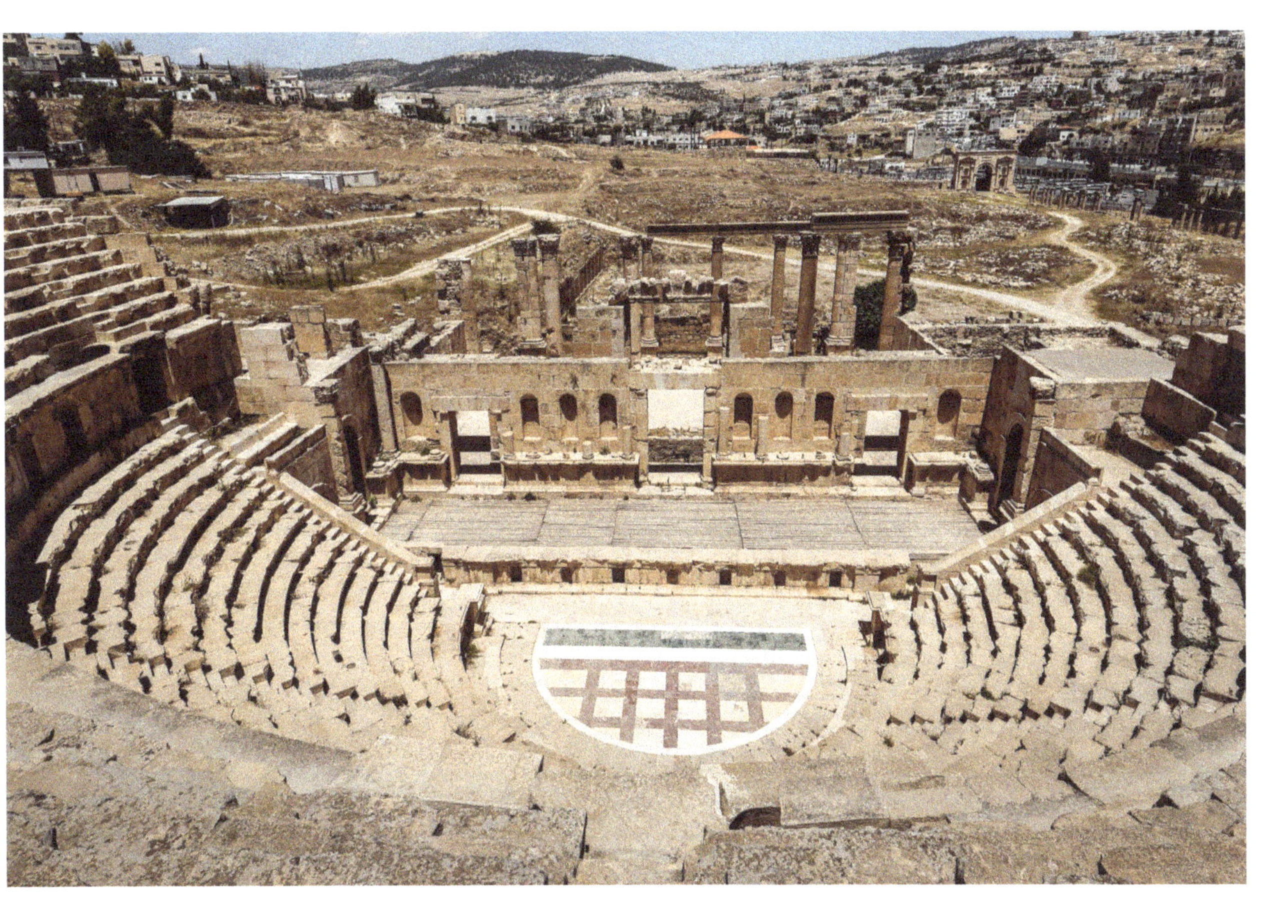

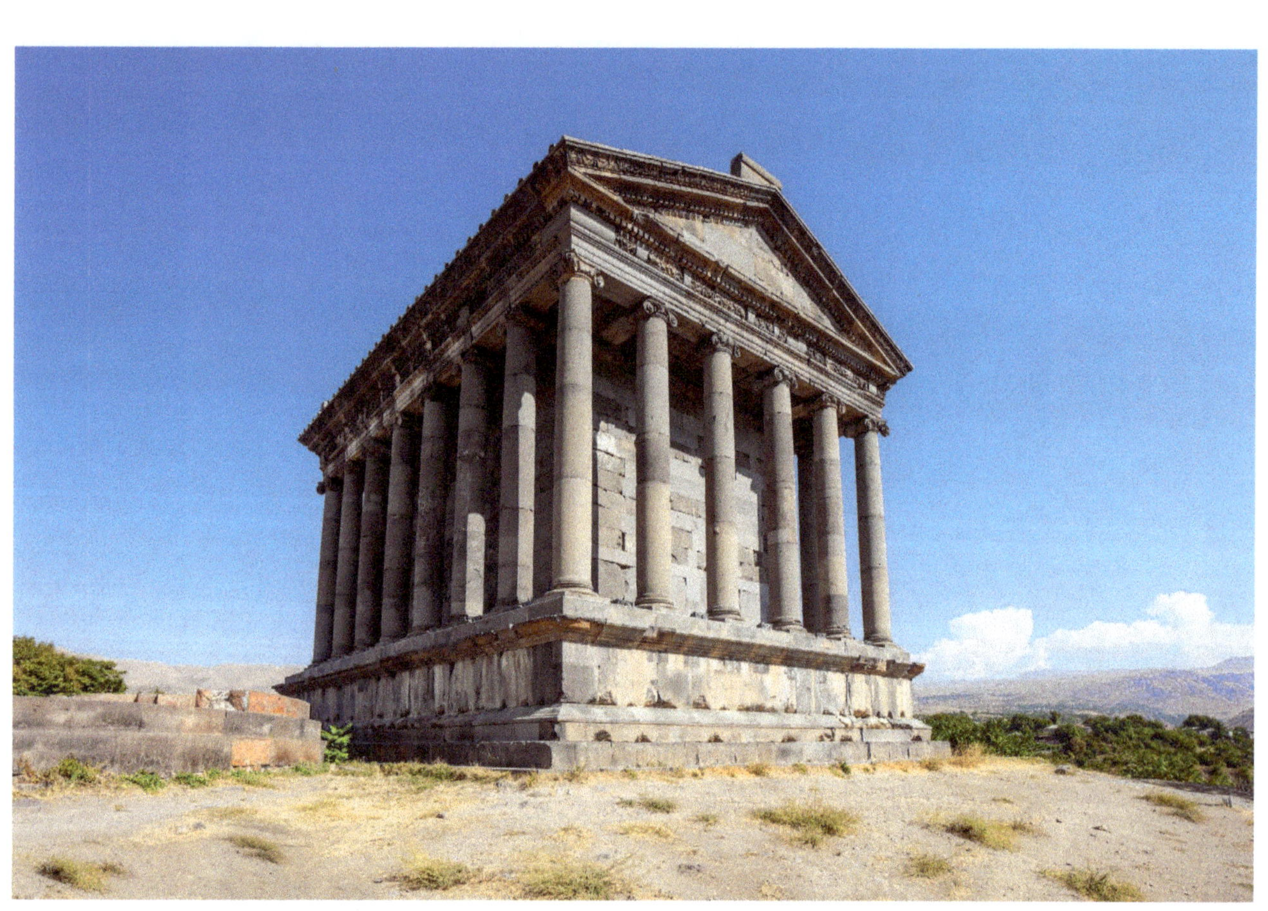

the early days of the Republic to the triumph of Christianity. Throughout Roman history the poor man struggles against the rich man, who holds him, first by war, then by games. But below the poor man there was a more miserable being who rarely saw the games, save as an actor in them. This was the slave, the dark rumbling of Suburra and the Catacombs, and woman, another slave, outraged every day and by all, in her flesh and in her tenderness. The being who lives in the shadows ceaselessly calls upon the sun to rise within him. The mystic tide of the poor, the tide born of Hellenic scepticism was mounting and was to submerge Roman materialism. Rome did not dream, doubtless, that the day on which she broke the frightful resistance of the little Jewish people marked the beginning of the victory of the little Jewish people over herself. It was in the law of things that the soul of the ancient world, compressed by Rome, should flow back into the soul of Rome. The patricians had been dominated by the Greek ideal; the plebeians, in their turn, were dominated by the Jewish ideal.

The church was to be built on this hard stone, and the rich man was again to enslave the poor man by giving him the promise, or the simulacrum, of the well-being to which he laid claim. Rome, by becoming Christian, did not cease to be herself; as she had remained Rome when she thought she had become Hellenistic. The apostles had already veiled the face of Christ. Rome had no trouble in casting the feeling of the masses in the mould of her will to launch them anew upon the conquest of the earth. Her material desire for world-empire was to reawaken upon coming into contact- with, the dream of universal moral communion, which Christianity, after faraway Buddhism, implanted in the souls of men; and it was to transform this dream to its profit. Julian the Apostate, the last hero who appeared on the dark earth before the fall of the sun, thought he was combating the religion of Asia. It was already against Rome that he was struggling, and Rome had the habit of conquering. The men of the north, flood after flood, may descend toward the Mediterranean, the great mirror of the divine figures, the inexhaustible basin of rays to which all the ancient peoples came to draw up light.

Rome, buried under incessant human waves for more than a thousand years, is to remain Rome, and when she reappears at the head of the peoples, the peoples are to perceive that they are marked with her imprint.

◀ *Temple of Garni* 1st century BC., Armenia.

▼ *Roman Forum.* Rome, Italy.

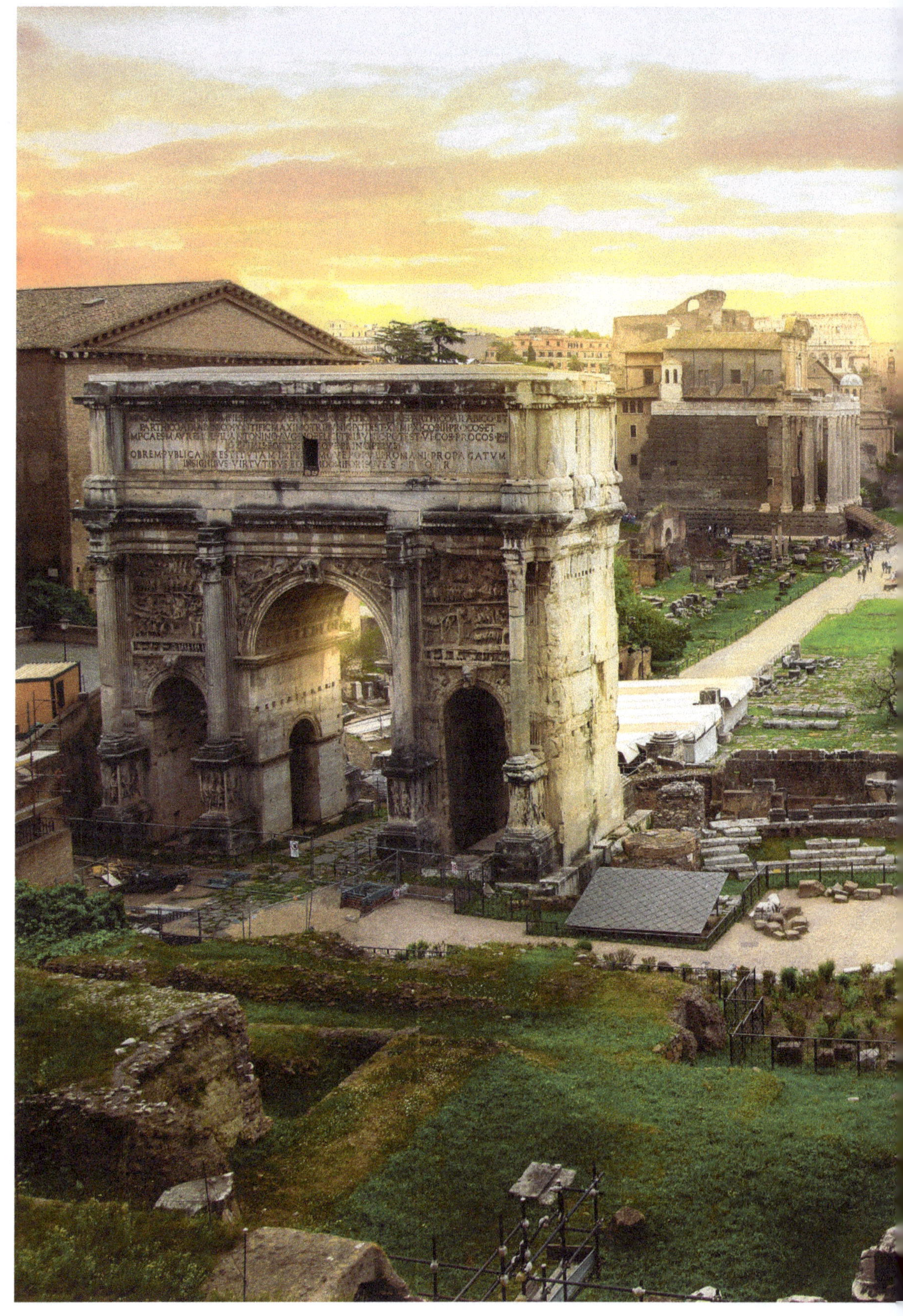

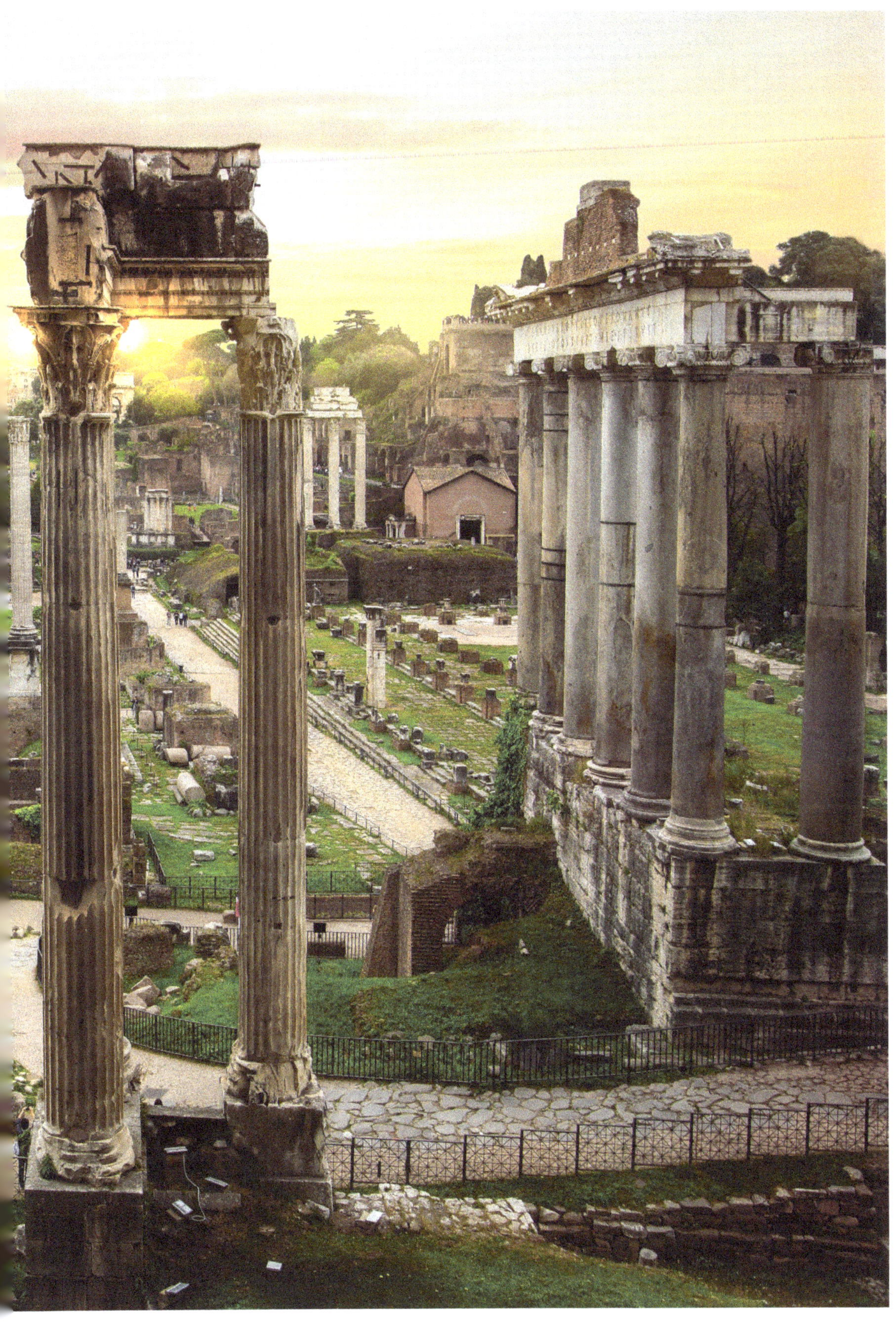

LIST OF ILLUSTRATIONS

ART HISTORY COLLECTION

Abstract Art

Art Deco

Art Nouveau

Baroque

Byzantine Art

Chinese Art

Cubism

Dada

Early Italian Art

Egypt Art

Expressionism

Gothic Art

Greek Art

Impressionism

Indian Art

Naive Art

Neoclassicism

Persian Art

Post-Impressionism

Realism

Renaissance

Pre-Raphaelites

Rococo

Roman Art

Romanesque Art

Romanticism

Surrealism

Symbolism

The Fauves

The Viennese Secession